THE ART OF
FORGIVENESS

Geiko Müller-Fahrenholz

THE ART OF FORGIVENESS

Theological Reflections on Healing and Reconciliation

WCC Publications, Geneva

A somewhat different version of this book was published in German as *Vergebung macht frei – Vorschläge für eine Theologie der Versöhnung,* © 1996 Verlag Otto Lembeck, Frankfurt am Main.
This English version © World Council of Churches, Geneva, 1997.

Cover design and symbol: Edwin Hassink

ISBN 2-8254-1224-4

© 1997 WCC Publications, World Council of Churches,
150 route de Ferney, 1211 Geneva 2, Switzerland

Printed in Switzerland

Table of Contents

Introduction

How dare I as a German talk about forgiveness? Fifty years have passed since the Nazis committed their atrocities against the Jewish people in Europe, against the Sinti and Roma, against members of opposition parties, religious activists and many other persons considered "unfit" for life; yet I know that Auschwitz is still painfully alive in the memories of many women and men. "Auschwitz" is the symbol of the systemic evil that continues to haunt all who have survived the Nazi era, the perpetrators and the victims alike, whether they can admit it or not. It also keeps haunting many who were born well after the second world war as they grapple with the question of how it was possible. What went wrong? How could a nation that was so respected a part of European civilization succumb to genocidal madness and seemingly unrestrained violence?

Born in 1940, I was too young to have conscious impressions of the Hitler period. But during my years at school and in university I wrestled with my horrible legacy. Like many women and men of my generation I felt the shame of being a German. As a matter of fact, I sometimes thought of emigrating to a country with a lighter history, say Canada or New Zealand (but how would the indigenous people of those countries react to my calling their history "light"?). As the years went by, I came to realize that it is foolish to run away from one's past. The only way forward was to face this ugly part of my country's history and to accept it along with the heavenly music of Johann Sebastian Bach and the beautiful poems of Hölderlin.

The more consciously I have moved along this road of hurt and shame, and the more I have been permitted to look into the unspeakable hurt and sadness of victimized people, the more I have been driven to the conclusion that it is necessary to think about forgiveness not *in spite of* Auschwitz but *because of* Auschwitz. There is no possibility of getting beyond such excesses of murderous violence other than by way of reconciliation.

Contemplating the meaning of forgiveness in light of the furnaces of Auschwitz requires a profound and relentless rereading of traditional Christian systematic and pastoral theology. Let me summarize at the outset the aspects I shall deal with extensively in this book:

1. Auschwitz forces us to reflect on forgiveness with the same intensity from the perspective of both the perpetrator and the victim. The Bible takes the victim's side when it looks at forgiveness. The way in which the Bible speaks about it indicates that *forgiveness of guilt and healing of suffering are inseparably bound together* in a process that heals the wounds of those who were humiliated as it heals the scars of those who abused their powers. This healing encounter opens up new and constructive alliances.

2. Just as I have "inherited" the atrocities of the Hitler era, so that the guilt of my parents' and grandparents' generations is my story, a similarly dark shadow hovers over the children and grandchildren of the victims; for the hurt and shame are carried over from one generation to the next, consciously and unconsciously. Any reflection on forgiveness must take seriously the complex historical impact of this guilt and this hurt: the inter-generational dimension which shows that *questions of forgiveness and reconciliation concern not only those directly involved but also those on whom the impact is "only" indirect*.

3. Auschwitz prohibits the reduction of guilt and shame to the individual level. Human beings act and fail to act not only as individual persons but also as members of families, associations, ethnic groups and nations. Similarly, they are also implicated in the collective experiences of families, groups and peoples. Hence forgiveness must also be studied as a public issue. As this book will show, forgiveness has a great deal to contribute to our understanding of politics, power, justice and renunciation. In the life of nations, the healing of memories of guilt and hurt is intimately linked to the building up of trusting alliances. *Those who want to go forward together need to walk through their histories together*.

4. Auschwitz makes it abundantly clear that *forgiveness can never replace justice*. Human codes of law establish indispensable rules of

life together and standards of relationships. Although all legal systems need constantly to be corrected and perfected, they constitute a fundamental achievement of the human race in its search for what is truly human. Any attempt to weaken the supremacy of the law thus entails the erosion of the humane. Forgiveness is about renouncing unjustified power, not about weakening the pursuit of justice.

The pursuit of justice within our prevailing legal systems is often a most frustrating exercise. In the case of the Nazi crimes only a relatively few perpetrators were found guilty; according to Rabbi Friedlander, in fewer than 6500 of the 90,000 cases brought to court was the accused convicted.[1] This fact remains alive in the memories of the surviving victims as an additional hurt.

More recently, the International Court in The Hague has been attempting to bring justice in the context of war-crimes committed in the former Yugoslavia. The exercise has been frustrating, since some of the most notorious criminals are walking about freely because it is politically inadvisable to bring them to court. Such impediments to justice present an additional barrier to our attempt to understand forgiveness; for they give rise to the suspicion that "forgiveness" is nothing but a nice word for "forgetfulness" and "pardon" a synonym of "amnesia".

5. At the same time, it must be emphasized that *forgiveness goes beyond justice*. While legal systems and procedures provide societies with reliable structures of punishment and protection, forgiveness strives to heal the grief and re-establish the deepest qualities of humanity.

Let me explain this briefly with a story that places the challenge of forgiveness in the context of Auschwitz. The story comes from Simon Wiesenthal, director of the Vienna-based Documentation Centre for Jews persecuted by the Nazi régime, well-known as the one who managed to track down Adolf Eichmann in Argentina and bring him to court in Jerusalem.

Wiesenthal's simple but moving story *Die Sonnenblume* (The Sunflower)[2] has many autobiographical connotations. It is set in the concentration camp of Lemberg, where Wiesenthal himself spent some years. One day the narrator is called to the bed of a 21-year-old member of the SS who is about to die and wishes to confess his murderous acts not to a priest, but to a Jew. Wiesenthal makes it quite clear that the confession of this young German is sincere. Torn between disgust and compassion, the narrator listens to the confession but leaves the room without speaking a word of absolution. The narrator then talks to his comrades in the camp about this incident — should he have forgiven? — but the answers of his fellow-prisoners do not satisfy him.

Wiesenthal then shared this story with Jewish and Christian theologians, philosophers, scientists and writers. Their responses, documented in the second part of "The Sunflower", are as moving as the story itself, because they reflect the same agonizing helplessness felt by the narrator. Some insist that the narrator was perfectly right to withhold forgiveness. Others are inclined to say that he ought to have found a pardoning word. But all agree that the request by the young German borders on the intolerable. How can a Jewish prisoner in a concentration camp become the father-confessor of a Nazi killer? Or, as a friend of the narrator puts it in the story, how can a *Herrenmensch* — a member of what the Nazis considered the superior race, the Aryan-German people — ask something superhuman from someone he would have thought of as an *Untermensch* — a member of one of the inferior, even subhuman peoples like the Jews and the Slavs?

Does this mean that forgiveness is something that goes beyond what is humanly possible? I want to suggest that the murderer, by way of his sincere confession, *disarms* himself and the prisoner is endowed with priestly powers. This means nothing less than that every process of genuine confession destroys the distorted relationships between human beings. The horrible distortion by which the Nazis had elevated themselves to *Herrenmenschen* and degraded so many others to *Untermenschen* is set right again: there are only *Menschen* — human beings!

In essence, the process of forgiveness aims at the restitution of the human. This is brought out clearly by the comment of a Dutch bishop, who writes that forgiving in this case "would have meant that *a human being* was prepared to accept the other, in spite of his terrible past, as *another human being*". That is why I believe that the search for forgiveness must continue *because of Auschwitz* if we want to keep on fighting for the deepest meaning of the human. "After having lost each other," says Rabbi Friedlander, "we have to find each other again *as human beings*."[3]

6. If our efforts at forgiveness aim at the human-ness of humanity, we are faced with the question: Who decides about this "human-ness"? What are the criteria for it and where do they come from? This leads me to a final paradoxical observation: *The quest for what is truly human transcends the human race.* In the last resort humans cannot define what constitutes their humanity. It transcends them.

There will be and must be many answers to these questions, but the one developed in this book is rooted in a part of the Jewish and Christian traditions which is shared by Islam. The holy scriptures of the Abrahamitic religions insist that the human-ness of the human race is grounded in the mercy of God. As we work for forgiveness, we are called to reflect that as human beings each of us is created in the image of God, the Most Merciful. This is our calling and mission: to become mirrors of mercy.

Bremen, January 1997   *Geiko Müller-Fahrenholz*

NOTES

[1] See A. Friedlander, *Das Ende der Nacht*, Gütersloh, 1995, p.224.
[2] I refer to the fifth edition of the German version, Berlin, Ullstein, 1993.
[3] *Op. cit.*, p.318 (italics added).

Part One

Mirrors of Mercy —
The Theological Basis

1. The Bible and Forgiveness

Reconciliation and forgiveness

Across the centuries and around the world, Christians confess their faith in the words of the ancient creeds, including "I believe in the forgiveness of sins". But what do Christians mean when they repeat this formula? How has it happened that "forgiveness" has become so devalued, even meaningless?

To reconstruct the meaning of forgiveness for people today we need to understand how it lapsed into irrelevance. This is a sad story; for in the Bible "forgiveness" is of paramount importance. So we shall look first at the biblical account of forgiveness, then reflect on how Christianity came to use — and to abuse — it.

We begin our brief exploration of what the Bible has to say about forgiveness by clarifying two terms that are often used interchangeably: reconciliation and forgiveness.

In general usage the term "reconciliation" is more widely used these days than forgiveness. It has the connotation of processes for correcting unjust or distorted situations. The theme of the second European Ecumenical Assembly (Graz 1997), "Reconciliation — God's Gift and Source of New Life", is a case in point. As the churches face the intense historical and contemporary divisions in Europe, the notion of reconciliation suggests processes of healing and restoration. The concept is applied not only to individuals, couples and families but also to social and ethnic groups and to entire nations. Hence it has become part of public rhetoric. Politicians have become fond of appealing for reconciliation, without of course indicating exactly how to bring it about.

In fact, this widespread use of the term is due to and in turn contributes to its lack of specificity. What is its content? Is it another word for peace, or harmony, or good-neighbourly relations? Reconciliation encompasses all these things but it tends to be spoken of in a way that suggests processes of getting somewhere without indicating what steps or conditions or procedures are involved and how they can be brought about.

The Latin root *concilium* suggests a deliberative process in which the conflicting partners meet each other "in council" to work out their differing views and to arrive at some common agreement. Yet we usually think of "reconciliation" as involving more than mere negotiation; it points towards some profound change in consciousness.

A good example is the Truth and Reconciliation Commission established by the transitional government of South Africa in 1995 to deal with some of the major human rights violations during the apartheid regime. We shall look more closely at this highly significant approach in chapter 12; here I mention it only to indicate that President Mandela's government considered it essential for the harmonious construction of a new and united South Africa explicitly to face the crimes and sufferings of the apartheid era. The Commission was set up to facilitate such a process of acknowledgment and healing.

It is revealing that the term "reconciliation" alone was considered inadequate to describe what was needed. The term "truth" was added. Perhaps this indicates that reconciliation by itself is considered too soft a notion to deal with the bitter memories of apartheid. At any rate it suggests that the term lacks the sharpness and clarity which is connoted by the term "truth".

When the term "forgiveness" is used these days, it generally seems to refer to a specific act of pardoning. Someone repents, someone forgives. "Repentance" and "forgiveness" are taken as the two sides of a process in which the perpetrator of an evil act confesses his or her remorse and the victim of that act grants pardon. Two elements explain why forgiveness has become so cheap a notion: its triteness and its inconsequentiality.

We have come to say "I'm sorry!" or "Excuse me!" for so many trifling things in everyday life that we no longer even wait for pardon. We take it for granted. We consider it an automatic response. The act of asking to be excused seems to imply its being granted. We are expected always to be ready to forgive. In other words, forgiveness has become a matter of politeness. It is nothing more than a social technique with which we smooth the rough edges of our daily hustle and bustle. As such this works quite well among "civilized" people. But we do not expect it to have any serious consequences for our behaviour. Since it costs so little to say "Pardon me!", we spend little time reflecting about how to avoid situations for which we need to excuse ourselves. In fact, the technique of expecting automatic pardon helps to justify our assumption that rude and offensive acts are normal.

The heart of the matter is that the element of guilt has almost completely vanished from this kind of "forgiveness". And the fact that we expect almost automatic pardon betrays another basic deficiency. We do not take seriously how the *victims* of our behaviour are feeling. The fixation on the actor's side leads us to overlook the impact of our actions on those who have to suffer them.

Compared to the vague and trivial usage of "reconciliation" and "forgiveness" today, the biblical account is surprising. "Reconciliation" occurs very sparingly. Only in Matthew 5:24 and 1 Corinthians 7:11 is the term used for relations between people; in all other references the Greek noun *katallagé* and verb *katallasso* are used exclusively for God's supreme act of reconciling humankind or the *kosmos* to God's self. Human beings are in no way actively involved; they are granted "reconciliation". The most concise summary of this understanding can be found in 2 Corinthians 5:17-21. The Greek term suggests a fundamental change, a complete renewal which only God can bring about. Therefore St Paul insists that "in Christ God was reconciling the world to himself... For our sake he made him to be sin who knew no sin, so that in him we might become the righteousness of God" (2 Cor. 5:19ff.). Reconciliation is thus a strictly theological concept, a supreme term to describe God's redeeming work.

In contrast, the term "forgiveness" (Greek, *aphesis*) is used widely in the Bible. The basic concept here is release from bondage, the remission of debt, guilt or punishment. Recall that in ancient times financial debts could lead to imprisonment or enslavement and that the redemption of such liabilities would mean liberation from prison or slavery for the debtor and his dependents.

In summary, the Bible understands forgiveness as a process which includes both the perpetrator and the victim. Forgiveness can occur when the perpetrator asks for it and the victim grants it. This mutuality is basic to an understanding of the biblical concept. Both sides are changed by this encounter. A healing takes place which paves the way for a better cooperation between formerly conflicting partners. Much more than a word or a gesture, forgiveness is a genuine process of encounter, of healing, of the releasing of new options for the future. A guilty and painful past is redeemed in order to establish reliable foundations for renewed fellowship in dignity and trust. Forgiveness frees the future from the haunting legacies of the past.

The notion of sin and the shift to the victim

Perhaps the best approach to the biblical concept of forgiveness is the recognition that there is nothing automatic about it. The Scriptures take the perspective of the victim seriously, which implies that they take the reality of guilt seriously.

The word for guilt we commonly find in our Bibles is "sin". Today, however, this word has lost its meaning for many people. They view sin as referring exclusively to one's relationship to God; and since God has become meaningless for them, sin is no longer a relevant concept. For the Bible, however, sin is an awful reality that exerts a profound influence on life in both social and transcendent ways. Sin against God invariably has an impact on the human being himself or herself, as well as on others and on the creation at large.

It is with fear and trembling that the Bible recognizes the profound mystery of this: how can the creatures of a merciful Creator be led to offend their Maker and to disrupt the beauty and peace of creation? When Cain kills his brother Abel (Gen. 4:1-16), it is not only the blood of the slain that cries out. The earth itself joins in this cry, and the heavens resonate with it. That is sin, an expression of rebellious violence which shakes creation to its core and hurts the very heart of God.

In the Hebrew Bible we find a twofold attempt to come to terms with this awe-inspiring and fateful reality. On the one hand, we see the people of the covenant struggling to elaborate commandments, rules and prohibitions in order to avoid sinful behaviour. The covenant with its law is understood as a merciful way to provide and secure a space for living at peace with God, with one's fellow human beings and with nature.

On the other hand, there is an awareness from the outset that even with the best intentions the best laws will be trespassed against. So an additional system of dealing with sin evolved, that of atonement. A priestly class was singled out and meticulous sacrificial rites were developed to secure atonement for those who perpetrated sinful deeds. The basic concept of the laws concerning offerings and sacrifices in the book of Leviticus is that the sin of a human being can be projected onto an animal, which then pays with its blood for the transgression of the one who offers it. There is considerable cathartic relevance in the scapegoat-ritual described in Leviticus 16:20ff.:

> [Aaron] shall present the live goat. Then Aaron shall lay both his hands on the head of the live goat, and confess over it all the iniquities of the people of Israel, and all their transgressions, all their sins, putting them on the head of the goat, and sending it away into the wilderness by means of someone designated for the task. The goat shall bear on itself all their iniquities to a barren region.

The accumulated violence of the community is projected onto a blameless goat, and the animal carries the sins of the people away into the wilderness. Thus is the integrity of the community restored.

At the basis of Israel's systems of law and expiation lies the awesome insight that the people's transgressions are painful to God and thus a great danger for the well-being of all of life. The Most High is hurt whenever the good ordinances of creation are violated. To put it even more pointedly, God is seen to be the victim of human violence and so God must be pacified lest all of creation vanish in vengeful fury.

Almost two thousand years have passed since the temple in Jerusalem was destroyed. The sacrifices have been abandoned or at least suspended; and the Jewish religion has cultivated insights — already voiced by the prophets — into the need to do justice rather than offer sacrifices. An eloquent example is found in the words of the prophet Amos:

> I hate, I despise your festivals,
> > and I take no delight in your solemn assemblies.
> Even though you offer me your burnt offerings and grain offerings,
> > I will not accept them;
> and the offerings of well-being of your fatted animals
> > I will not look upon...
> But let justice roll down like waters,
> > and righteousness like an ever-flowing stream (Amos 5:21-24).

Justice and not sacrifice! This is the basis on which Jewish theologians have defined the Jewish faith as an ethical religion. Rabbi Albert Friedlander says that "the special revelation of the Jewish religion, its singular contribution to the world, lies in the ethical"; and he cites Leo Baeck's statement that "ethics constitute the principle of Jewish-ness, its essence". [1] So atonement is absorbed into faithfulness: the mystery of God's faithfulness and human rebellion is met by living according to the Torah, the blessed Law of God.

Christianity, although deeply grounded in and eternally indebted to the Jewish faith, has taken a markedly different turn. It is the central importance of Jesus as the Messiah that accounts for the paradigmatic shift from a religion of the law to a religion of love — to use Pauline categories. The Christian faith centres on the cross and resurrection of Jesus. In the life and death of this Jew, Christianity sees the victim-God who offers unconditional forgiveness to all who will believe. The New Testament letter to the Hebrews concentrates on this paradigmatic shift, placing the saving work of Jesus in contrast to the atoning structures of the Jewish temple. So it describes Jesus as both the perfect high priest and the blameless sacrifice — "the Lamb of God who takes away the sins of the world" (John 1:29). The fundamental critique of the scapegoating mechanism found in the Hebrew Bible has appeared again and again within Christianity as well. The letter to the Ephesians puts it this way: Christ has abolished the hostility that ruled the world in his body on the cross. The violence is overcome; the temple of God is being built up in the midst of God's creation (Eph. 2:11-22).

This soteriological shift is brought out most clearly in Jesus' prayer from the cross: "Father, forgive them; for they do not know what they are doing" (Luke 23:34). The victimized Son intercedes for the world to the victim-God, pleading for forgiveness; for we, the human race, do not know that our violence — our sin — is breaking the heart of God and tearing the world apart.

So the Christian faith as proclaimed in the New Testament may well be understood as a religion which centres on forgiveness. Thus it is appropriate that the forgiveness of sins is placed in the article of the ancient creeds which deals with the Holy Spirit, for the Holy Spirit signifies the presence of God as revealed in the Son in all of history and creation. It is the presence of the energy of eternal and unremitting love, the very storm of mercy (the Hebrew word for "spirit", *ruach*, literally means breath and storm). In this presence of the *ruach* we are called to become children of God and friends to each other.

The placement of the forgiveness of sins in the ancient creeds attests further to the raison d'être of the church. The only thing that is said about the earthly mission of the one, holy, catholic and apostolic church is this: that sins should be forgiven, that violence should be met with love and enmity with unfailing compassion. It may thus be said that the church is called into being in order to witness to forgiveness as liberation and pacification in the face of a world at war with itself. This is pointed to by the familiar New Testament images of the church as the kingdom of heaven, the body of Christ, the new Jerusalem. To a world divided, all portray the great alternative of peace.

I want to emphasize that this is not an anti-Jewish argument. We shall see in subsequent chapters that the church has no reason whatever to set itself above the synagogue; for during most of its life it has neither understood nor incorporated the example of its Lord. Regardless of what the early creeds affirm, Christian communities have betrayed the central message of the Good News, to the extent that Christianity has rightly been called one of the bloodiest and most violent religions the world has ever seen. The betrayal set in early, with the repeated attempts to blame the Jews for the crucifixion of Jesus — a clear indication that the church retained the scapegoating mechanism which Jesus came to overcome. As Gil Bailie has observed, "The crucifixion's anthropological significance is lost if responsibility for its violence is shifted from *all* to *some*. To lay the blame on the Pharisees or the Jews is to undermine the universal meaning of the crucifixion in favour of the familiar theory of human wickedness."[2] But this is exactly what happened.

NOTES

[1] A.H. Friedlander, *Leo Baeck: Teacher of Theresienstadt*, New York, Holt, Rinehart & Winston, 1968.

[2] Gil Bailie, *Violence Unveiled: Humanity at the Crossroads*, New York, Crossroad, 1995, p.218.

2. Distortions in Church History

To explain why Christianity failed to grasp the meaning of forgiveness as revealed in Christ it is not adequate simply to appeal to the general pattern of sacred violence identified by anthropologists, although its contagious power is ever-present. It seems to me that three major elements account for the perversion of the biblical notion of forgiveness in church history: the abuse of forgiveness as an instrument of ecclesiastical power-politics, the privatization and "verticalization" of forgiveness, and the traditional fixation on the perpetrator rather than the victim.

Controlling the keys to the kingdom: forgiveness as a tool of power-politics

Perhaps no biblical text has suffered more radical misinterpretation than Matthew 16:18-19: "You are Peter, and on this rock I will build my church, and the gates of Hades will not prevail against it. I will give you the keys of the kingdom of heaven, and whatever you bind on earth will be bound in heaven, and whatever you loose on earth will be loosed in heaven."

The context makes it abundantly clear that the "keys of the kingdom of heaven" are given to those who follow the Crucified (v.21) and accept taking up his cross as a mark of their discipleship (v.24). The power to bind and to loose — that is, the power to grant and to withhold forgiveness — is promised to those who are prepared to lose their lives for Christ's sake (v.25) and who do not try to "gain the whole world" (v.26).

During the first decades the "keys of the kingdom" were a dangerous gift to the persecuted Christian communities. But when the Emperor Constantine the Great turned the cross of the Victim-God into a symbol of the triumphant Victor-God, the commission to bind and to loose turned into a fabulous instrument of earthly power. Especially the bishops of Rome, who claimed ultimate papal authority as Christ's "vicar on earth", learned to exercise this power with often ruthless sophistication.

Perhaps the most vivid example in European history of the impact of forgiveness as an instrument of power-politics is that of Emperor Henry IV, obliged in 1077 to stand barefooted and wearing a hair shirt in the court of Canossa for a full three days before Pope Gregory VII was disposed to accept his penitence, lift his excommunication and end his banning. Henry's "march to Canossa" is remembered as the epitome of humiliation. To be sure, it can and must also be seen as a shrewd power-play between two political rivals, but the salient point here is the abuse of the idea of forgiveness.

Control of the keys of the kingdom turned the disciples of Jesus, who were meant to be "workers for the joy" of the people into "lords over their faith" (2 Cor. 1:24). As long as people could be persuaded that they needed God's presence to sustain their lives and the sacraments of the church in order not to end up in eternal damnation, the religious institutions could hold on to supreme power. By threatening to bind the sinner on earth and in heaven, the sacrament of penance (into which the gospel of forgiveness had been transformed) became an instrument of religious terror, rendering the priests, bishops and popes absolute masters over the people's consciences and lives. And, as is well-known, this spiritual power generated tremendous material and political gains.

It was this distortion of the gospel of forgiveness that caused the division of the church in the West during the 16th century. Significantly, the first of Martin Luther's famous 95 theses, whose posting on the door of the church in Wittenberg on the eve of All Saints Day in 1517 is commonly considered to mark the beginning of the Reformation, deals critically with the then-prevailing penitential practice: "When our Lord and Master Jesus Christ said, 'Repent' (Matt. 4:17), he willed the entire life of believers to be one of repentance."

This thesis encapsulates the Reformers' attempt to destroy the pervasive and complicated network of penitential practices by presenting repentance as a lifelong condition. This generalization corresponds with Luther's radical understanding of sin as a lifelong condition of estrangement from God. This understanding of sin as an existential predicament led him vigorously to oppose any attempt to divide it into categories of "lighter", "heavier" and "deadly" sins.

Article 12 of the Augsburg Confession (1530) maintains that genuine penitence consists of two elements: contrition — the sincere acknowledgment of the depth of the sinful condition — and the faith that by the grace of God all sins are forgiven. The element of good works is played down, for fear of betraying the pure "justification by faith":

> It is taught among us that those who sin after baptism receive forgiveness of sin whenever they come to repentance, and absolution should not be denied them by the church.
>
> Properly speaking, true repentance is nothing else than to have contrition and sorrow, or terror, on account of sin, and yet at the same time to believe the gospel and absolution (namely that sin has been forgiven and grace has been obtained through Christ), and this faith will comfort the heart and again set it at rest. Amendment of life and the forsaking of sin should then follow, for these must be the fruits of repentance...
>
> Rejected are those who teach that forgiveness of sin is not obtained through faith but through the satisfactions made by man. [1]

The rapid spread of the Reformation through Europe was no doubt related to its fervent critique of the church's abuses of penance, which destroyed the enormously oppressive power it derived from the fear of tormented consciences. In fact, this power was now recognized as a perversion of Christ's gospel, and thus the popes were regarded as instruments of the Anti-Christ. The Reformation was welcomed as a liberation from religious oppression.

Although the Roman Catholic Church managed through the Counter-Reformation to reclaim large regions of Europe, it was never able to re-establish the sacrament of penance as a means to control the consciences of women and men. People in Europe had become deeply suspicious of any form of religious power. The penitential terror of the Dark Ages led to a profound disillusionment with the ministries of the church — a process which hastened the advance of secularization. The "keys of the kingdom" had been embezzled.

The verticalist reduction

The intention of the Reformation was to regain the biblical understanding of sin and the good news of forgiveness. So the Reformers stressed the pervasiveness of sin in order to affirm that genuine deliverance could come only from God and through "grace alone". A famous hymn by Luther is typical of this approach:

'Tis through Thy love alone we gain the pardon of our sin;
the strictest life is but in vain, our works can nothing win;
that none should boast himself of aught,
but own in fear Thy grace has wrought
what in him seemeth righteous.
Wherefore my hope is in the Lord,
my works I count but dust (*"Aus tiefer Not"*, tr. C. Winkworth).

This radicalization of sin corresponds to the radical concentration on Christ and his redeeming work which made "Christ alone!" (*solus Christus*) the battle-cry of the Reformation. Because of Christ (*propter Christum*) forgiveness of sin is ours by faith.

While this emphasis clearly reflects the basic message of the New Testament, its weakness is that it accentuates the vertical dimension in our understanding of forgiveness — that having to do with the relationship between the believer and God — as distinct from his or her horizontal relationships to other human beings, society and nature. This verticalist reduction of sin to the immediate relationship between the faithful and God meant that any consideration of its effect and impact in the social and natural realms could easily be dismissed as a question of "law" and shunned as a typically "Catholic" preoccupation. This placed the sinner at the centre of theology and spirituality, not the one who is sinned-against, the victim of sin. What mattered most was what sin does to God. What it does to God's world appeared peripheral.

This reductionism led to the privatization and spiritualization of sin and forgiveness. To be sure, when Article 11 of the Augsburg Confession mentions *absolutio privata* and when the Reformers insisted on "private confession", it was not just a reflection of a radical understanding of sin; it was also intended to lead the church back to its original mission of preaching the undeserved grace of God and to abolish the public administration of absolution with its political and economic abuses. However, the tendency to privatize sin and forgiveness gave way to a spiritualization — or rather a de-materialization — of what sin and forgiveness imply. The social, political and economic implications of these central notions of the faith became difficult to detect; and eventually a dual approach evolved which came to be systematized as the "two-kingdoms doctrine" (*Zweireichelehre*). It left the concerns of salvation, including forgiveness, to the realm of the gospel, whereas the concerns of the "world", including economics and politics, belonged to the realm of the law. [2]

Another weakness in the verticalization of forgiveness became apparent only much later — particularly in the 20th century. We can sum it up in this question: What happens to a strictly vertical concept when the reality to which this line points disappears, when God is declared dead? The critique of religion formulated by Feuerbach, Marx and many others insisted that God is a mere human projection and that people's concerns about salvation and divine pardon are religious needs derived from social and economic want. This critical atheism has paved the way for the practical godlessness of contemporary Western societies, the almost complete loss of accountability to a transcendental being. The only dimension remaining seems to be the horizontal; the vertical relationship, if it is admitted at all, is bereft of any practical meaning.

If there is no God to whom I owe my being and to whom I am accountable, then it makes no sense at all to talk about sin. Where there is no God, there is no sin. And where there is no sin, there is no need for forgiveness.

The fixation on the sinner

It is revealing that in many European languages "to sin" can be used only as an active verb; the passive form is grammatically impossible. We "sin", but when we are the object of such activity we can only say that we "suffer sin" or "are sinned against". Apparently, "to sin" is a way of behaving which knows only subjects but no objects.

This grammatical observation reveals a significant trait in the European consciousness, namely that of placing the sinner in the centre of attention. What sinners do to their fellow human beings or to creation at large is of secondary relevance. The verticalist reduction favoured a fixation on those who committed sin, not on those who suffered it. This preoccupation with the sinner shines through count-less hymns and litanies and doctrinal statements.

It is an achievement of liberation theology to have introduced a corrective element here. Liberation theologians insist in doing theol-ogy from the perspective of the poor, and in so doing they recapture the biblical worldview which brings the victim to the centre of theological attention. Certainly they would agree that "sin" is a condition which separates us from God, but they insist that this fact conditions our lives by creating suffering, pain and injustices of many kinds. Sin is therefore both a vertical and a horizontal reality; and it must be studied both as a theological and as a social category. Sin is not so much an ontological construct that describes our primordial fallen-ness, but an historical category that depicts what we do and suffer. Sin manifests itself in history as violence.

This then creates an opportunity to affirm the harsh reality of human suffering and guilt. People may wish to deny that God exists, but they cannot ignore that there is guilt. If that is the case, the notion of forgiveness must attain a social, economic and political dimension as well. It cannot be reduced to a "thin" religious affirmation but needs to be seen as a power that liberates people from the violence and victimization they heap on each other. So the forgiving mercy of God translates itself into forbearance and magnanimity towards others and towards oneself. Those who are liberated by the grace of God will strive to set others free.

Does this then bring us back to the old debate about "good works"? No and yes. Bear in mind that the traditional discussion about good works took place within the confines of what we have called the fixation on the perpetrator. By their good deeds sinners were meant to prove the sincerity of their repentance, not to heal the damage done to victims. At a strictly theological level, however, good works make no sense; for no one can earn the forgiving grace of God, which is free.

But if we look at the problem of sin and good works from the victims' point of view the matter changes radically. For those who are humiliated, exploited and abused, it makes a great deal of difference whether or not the sinners stop doing their evil deeds and whether or not they attempt to heal the wounds their greed and violence have opened. From this perspective, it is extremely significant that the gospels speak not only of the redeeming death of Christ on the cross, but also tell in considerable detail the stories of Jesus healing sick people, liberating those who were possessed, feeding hungry crowds, even raising persons from the dead. These stories are meant to teach us that Jesus identified with the victims. He took their side. So when Jesus forgives sins, he unburdens those who are heavy laden. He sets the captives free. He eats with the outcasts and seeks their company. Indeed, it was this taking the side of the victims that most irritated and angered the authorities of his day. Jesus was put to death because he was on the wrong side.

If we take seriously the orientation to the victim, it is by no means foolish to talk about good deeds. In fact the New Testament does this with great urgency. It speaks about the good fruits by which a good tree can be recognized (Matt. 7:16). And these fruits are not religious or cultic practices but (to cite Paul) "love, joy, peace, patience, kindness, generosity, faithfulness, gentleness and self-control" (Gal. 5:22) — tangible virtues which have a direct bearing on how people live and work together. In such ways the Spirit of the Crucified is present among the faithful. So the keys to the kingdom of heaven become workable, though often distorted, tools in the impasses and agonies of real life. Forgiveness of sins, therefore, becomes manifest as liberation from oppression, as healing of pain, as critique of self-righteous power, as pacification of destroyed relationships.

In contrasting this option for the victim with the prevailing fixation on the sinner, we come to see once again why forgiveness has lost its meaning for many people. Traditional Christian teaching and spirituality — both Catholic and Protestant — tended to address only the sinner and lost sight of the many who were "sinned against". Because it was thus unable to appreciate the dimension of suffering and hurt that sin inflicts on so many people, it was also unable to witness to the uplifting, restoring and liberating power of forgiveness. The betrayal of those who suffer has contributed to the fact that the gospel of forgiveness has become "cheap grace", to use Dietrich Bonhoeffer's phrase. It is time, therefore, to reconstruct its life-giving and life-restoring value.

NOTES

[1] The final dogmatic form of the sacrament of penance in the Middle Ages distinguished three stages: (1) heartfelt contrition (*contritio cordis*); (2) explicit oral confession (*confessio oris*); and (3) the satisfaction manifested in some work or ritual practice (*satisfactio operis*). The intent of this third element remained somewhat ambivalent. On the one hand, it was stressed that God does not need "good deeds" as proof of the sinner's heartfelt repentance, although they were considered a sign of sincerity. On the other hand, the idea of expiation and recompensation played a role, so that "good deeds" could be seen as a means by which the sinners could "make good" for their transgressions.

[2] On this see F. Lau, *Zweireichelehre*, in *Die Religion in Geschichte und Gegenwart*, 3rd ed., Tübingen, J.C.B. Mohr, Vol. 6, cols 1945-49.

3. Futile Approaches to Guilt

Although many women and men today have a rather confused grasp of sin, they know — even if they may hesitate to admit it — what guilt is and how it feels to be a victim. As a matter of fact the violence of perpetrators and the cries of victims reverberate throughout the world. No one can deny that people do evil and suffer evil. But since so many people no longer have a God or a devil to whom to attribute their predicament, it has become exceedingly difficult to come to terms with it. How can we interpret the reality of forgiveness in ways our contemporaries can understand? It will have to be a "non-religious" or "worldly" interpretation, to use Bonhoeffer's much-disputed term, that is, one which tries to stay within the conceptual and experiential framework of contemporary secularized life. [1]

Everything that has to do with guilt and suffering goes to the very core of our being. So I propose to approach it inductively by looking first at three inadequate approaches that are common to us all.

Trivialization: guilt as error

We referred earlier to the tendency to trivialize forgiveness by turning it into a form of politeness. We said that this corresponds with the trend to trivialize guilt. Now we must take a closer look at this phenomenon.

Most people are prepared to admit that they make mistakes. *Errare humanum est* — "to err is human" — is a piece of common wisdom that dates back to Roman times. Errors are unavoidable. As a matter of fact, by making mistakes we learn to do things better. It is of course unfortunate that whenever one makes a mistake some other person might have to suffer, but this cannot be avoided. In such cases one is expected to excuse oneself and to repair the damage if necessary or possible. It is expected that the victim will accept the excuse almost automatically, for he or she might soon be in a similar situation.

There is no denying that this principle of "error and excuse" functions well in many circumstances. There are many trespasses that follow from unintentional errors and miscalculations. So it is only right that there should be mechanisms of repair and compensation to help correct the situation.

Mistakes are actions we commit without malice or evil intentions. But we know full well that there is another range of actions and omissions which cannot be subsumed under this category. These are the things we do — or do not do — intentionally and by which we purposefully seek to achieve some impact, be it good or evil. It must be conceded, of course, that human beings are by no means always aware or in control of their intentions, motivations and impulses. But this does not permit us to trivialize such actions to the level of unconscious "errors". If we wish to be regarded as human beings, as subjects who can say "I", we have to admit that we can and do become guilty. As conscious human beings we give and receive love, and in the same way we become guilty and suffer guilt at the hands of others. Guilt is a product of human consciousness and social interaction.

To deny the reality of guilt is to deny one of the most profound and disturbing aspects of our humanity. We impoverish ourselves if we reduce this to mere human frailty. Human beings are more than conglomerates of unconscious motives and uncontrollable passions. To admit our guiltiness is a matter of honesty and dignity.

Fighting guilt with guilt: the downward spiral of revenge

The formula "an eye for an eye" sums up the atavistic mechanism of revenge. Although commonly despised as an archaic barbarism from bygone ages, the practice of revenge is alive in many parts of the world today. Cases of vendetta lock feuding families, clans or ethnic groups in a murderous embrace, sometimes to the point of total exhaustion. We read about entire villages in Sicily where the men in feuding families are caught in the iron fist of mutual destruction till only women in black clothes remain alive to mourn the dead. Yet there is also something awfully honest about this, for whenever people resort to revenge guilt is acknowledged. The horror of a crime is faced with deadly sincerity.

"Whoever sheds the blood of a human, by a human shall that person's blood be shed" (Gen. 9:6) reflects the profound conviction that blood is the sacred bearer of life and that it is a heinous attack on life itself to spill it. Those who take another person's life put themselves outside the rightful course of history. They must be killed as well lest they become a curse for the order of things. So revenge is about maintaining an equity of horror.

Revenge is also about maintaining an equity of suffering. There must be a gruesome compatibility of guilt and suffering on both sides. The scales must be balanced. Each party in a vendetta must share the same suffering. The perpetrator must be made into a victim while the victim becomes a perpetrator.

This attempt to establish an equitable level of "dignity" must be called an act of despair, because it meets violence with violence. Moreover, it turns into a cult of violence because no attempt is made to heal or in any way transcend the suffering, only to replicate it. Within a culture of revenge nobody believes that the fateful mechanism of violence can be broken or suspended. The only course that seems open is to step more and more deeply into guilt. And so the downward spiral of violence is fixed.

A revealing example of this downward spiral of violence is found in the mythic story of Lamech, whose horrendous song we read in Genesis 4:23f.:

> Lamech said to his wives:
> Adah and Zillah, hear my voice...,
> listen to what I say:
> I have killed a man for wounding me,
> a young man for striking me.
> If Cain is avenged sevenfold,
> truly Lamech seventy-sevenfold.

When Jesus is asked by his disciples whether it is enough to forgive someone seven times (in contrast to Cain), he replies: "Not seven times, but, I tell you, seventy-seven times" (Matt. 18:21f.). So Jesus places his message of forgiveness in contrast to the vengeful violentism of Lamech.

It may seem odd to give so much attention to revenge in a book about forgiveness. But it is important to look at this gruesome mechanism because it tells us a great deal about the reality of guilt and the massive impact of victimization. Moreover, in our disgust with the unconcealed atavism of classic vendettas, we should not overlook the fact that much of present-day power-politics employs rather similar mechanisms, though sanitized with the name "retaliation" rather than "revenge".

Looking at the terrible "logic" of revenge helps us to get a clearer impression of the magnitude of forgiveness, which is not an exercise in pious romanticism but a challenge of staggering proportions.

In the courts of justice

The most important instrument our societies have developed to deal with guilt and victimization is the legal system. I would not hesitate to say that the highest achievement of civilized nations is to take the prosecution and punishment of criminal acts out of the hands of those directly involved and to submit it to the judiciary, to replace the atavistic and self-destructive mechanism of revenge by publicly regulated mechanisms of justice. The legal system is designed to meet various public interests, notably the punishment and seclusion of criminal offenders and if possible their "resocialization", the compensation of the victim for incurred damage or loss and not least the protection of the public from criminal activity.

But if we ask whether the judiciary can deal satisfactorily with guilt and victimization, the answer must be No. Although it is an indispensable instrument for providing some measure of order and stability to society, it can never hope to meet guilt and victimization at its deepest level. Consider, for example, the issue of compensation. In many cases such attempts border on the obscene. With murder this is obvious, but it applies also to criminal offences like rape or child abuse, in which material compensation can easily appear to be an additional humiliation.

This is even more so in regard to collective crimes. We mentioned in the introduction that more than 90 percent of the 90,000 cases filed against Nazi criminals in the Federal Republic of Germany ended in acquittal. Obviously the courts considered the evidence against these persons inconclusive. This caused considerable frustration among the surviving victims of the Nazi era, adding to their bitterness and raising the suspicion that the German judiciary had not really freed itself from anti-Semitism. [2]

Although there are some compelling examples that would support this suspicion, I do not think that it is generally true. Rather, there is something in all judiciary systems that frustrates the victims. This has to do with the basic preoccupation of the law with the criminal offenders and their deeds. *In dubio pro reo* ("in doubt decide for the accused") is a maxim dating back to Roman law. This "presumption of innocence" substantiates the point I am trying to make. Our judicial systems are marked by the same "sinner-fixation" which we observed in the theological field. There is a good reason why this should be so, but the inevitable side-effect is that the victims often feel left out of the case. The administration of justice centres on the punishment of the culprit, and it is simply assumed that this is also the way in which the pain and hurt of the victim will be healed — which is of course an illusion.

This is the great significance of the terms of reference of the South African Truth and Reconciliation Commission; for this body (which we shall look at in greater detail in chapter 12) is requested to listen to the accounts of the victims first. The hearings of the Commission follow quasi-judicial procedures and yet they work in a manner which differs markedly from traditional courts. Attention is directed towards unearthing the truth by listening with care and empathy to the witnesses. This clear orientation towards the victims achieves something the courts cannot do: contribute to restoring the dignity of the victims. The emphasis is not on punishment, but on healing.

The South African approach is unprecedented; and it is useful to compare it with how collective war crimes and human rights violations have been tried elsewhere. For me as a German, the South African initiative throws new light on how my own country has attempted to come to terms with the Nazi past. Besides the court cases already mentioned, governments of the Federal Republic have tried since the second world war to compensate for crimes committed during the Nazi régime:

> The Federal Republic made [financial restitution] to people in all the Nazi-occupied nations who could prove that their occupiers had robbed them or inflicted gross suffering upon them. Included in these measures... was a DM 3000 million payment to Israel, plus hundreds of millions more in compensation to individual Jews who had survived the

Holocaust. Through 1986, the Bonn government settled some four-and-a-half million such personal claims for a total of some US$40,000 million. The several compensation laws of this latter decade laid down provisions that by the year 2000, according to a 1988 government document, international payments in excess of... some US$70,000 million would have been made. [3]

These efforts are respectable; yet they did not and could not heal the hurt of surviving victims — not to mention the bitterness felt by Sinti and Roma people, whose claims for restitution were never admitted. Money simply cannot restore the humiliation and pain of those who were made to suffer unspeakable injustices.

In this context it is revealing that after all these years Germany has yet to build a national holocaust museum, although many regional memorials exist. So far it has proved too difficult to agree on a central holocaust memorial in the capital of Berlin. Why is this? Have German governments tried to hide behind their restitution payments in order not to listen to the pain of the victims?

The South African experience suggests new ways of bringing justice to the land, not only by punishing the perpetrators or making amends to the victims, but by consciously restoring the dignity of humiliated persons.

One final observation. The judicial system can deal with only a tiny fraction of the guilt and hurt that burden the people. A great deal of injustice cannot and will never be brought to court. A marriage can be a guilt-ridden affair without ever reaching the courthouse. This leads to the remark that guilt and hurt are perceived very differently in different situations. It seems to me that in most cases the corresponding category to guilt and hurt is not justice, but love or trust. One can become very guilty by betraying the love or confidence of a spouse or a family member without ever breaking any laws.

Our references to dignity, love and trust indicate that guilt and hurt have an impact on the very core of our being. They affect our identity as persons. This explains why in the last resort the depth of guilt and the burning agonies of hurt can never be met by the trivialization of guilt or by the violentism of revenge or even by the pursuit of justice. We have to dig deeper.

NOTES

[1] See *Letters and Papers from Prison*, tr. R.H. Fuller, New York, Macmillan, 1962, esp. the letter of 16 July 1944, pp.215-20.

[2] See Ralph Giordano, *Die Zweite Schuld oder Von der Last Deutscher zu sein* ("The Second Guilt, or About the Burden of Being German"), Hamburg, 1987.

[3] Donald Shriver, *An Ethic for Enemies: Forgiveness in Politics*, Oxford and New York, Oxford UP, 1995, p.89.

4. *Setting Each Other Free*

To understand what forgiveness does to our relationships we need to see the bondage that evil creates. In *Song of Solomon* the African-American novelist Toni Morrison writes, "If you take a life, then you own it. You responsible for it. You can't get rid of nobody by killing them. They are still there, and they yours now." This is a forceful way of saying that every act of transgression constitutes a bondage that keeps the perpetrator and the victim locked together. The more violent the transgression, the deeper the bondage.

The philosopher Hannah Arendt points out that transgressions cannot be avoided. They are daily occurrences which follow from the nature of human activity. We cannot be active beings without getting in someone else's way. Relationships are helpful, but they can also be hurtful. Our look can be respectful of another person; it can also be intruding. Words can make someone laugh or cry. An embrace can heal, an embrace can kill. So Arendt says that humans need ways constantly to disentangle themselves from hurtful and compromising relationships:

> It needs forgiving, dismissing, in order to make it possible for life to go on by constantly releasing men from what they have done unknowingly. Only through this constant mutual release from what they do can men remain free agents. [1]

Earlier, we spoke of the many trivial ways in which we excuse ourselves from the petty transgressions that occur in our daily lives. But it is also apparent that the heavier the guilt and the more painful the hurt, the more difficult this mutual unburdening becomes. Of course, it is possible to learn to live with such bondage. We are familiar with the techniques by which perpetrators silence their consciences and muffle every trace of remorse. Psychologists have described the power of "numbing", which enables people to create what Freud called a "protective shield" around all kinds of threatening feelings. [2] People manage somehow to forget the wrongs they have done; similarly, victims learn to live with their traumatic hurts. But it is well-known that extended forms of repression and denial lead to distortions of character and illnesses of various kinds.

Evil acts create chains that lock perpetrators and victims together, usually in unconscious ways, producing a double history of effects (*Wirkungsgeschichte*) which must be taken into account in reflecting on the nature of forgiveness. An act of forgiveness must be understood as a complex process of "unlocking" painful bondage, of mutual liberation. While the perpetrators must be set free from their guilt (and its devastating consequences), the victims must be liberated from their hurt (and its destructive implications). This mutual liberation implies a process of catharsis, and this is the point which scares most people. Much as they might long to be freed from their bondage, they shy away from entering into this cathartic moment. Why? What they dread is the process of dismantling and exposure.

The German term *Entblössung* (literally, "denuding oneself") describes something the traditional word "repentance" no longer conveys. It identifies a process by which one returns to the point at which the original evil act was done. To revisit this moment implies admitting all the shameful implications of that act. It is painful to enter into this shame. It is more painful still to acknowledge this act in the face of those who suffered it. All confessions of guilt carry with them an element of self-humiliation which runs counter to our pride and seems to threaten our self-esteem. Nobody likes to be stripped of his or her defences and to appear naked in front of others.

To avoid the panic and horror this process of dismantling creates, people go to extremes. They will hold on to denial even if their guilt is there for all to see. They will rationalize their act, play it down or inculpate others. Since acknowledging guilt appears to be an unforgivable weakness, barricades of spite or self-righteousness are frantically thrown up.

Such well-known manoeuvres help us to appreciate the kind of strength required to enter into the pain of *Entblössung*. This is not something for cowards: it demands great courage and self-esteem. To lay oneself open is nothing less than an act of disarmament. You put down the weapons you employed to dominate others; you renounce the power you gained by stealing it from the victim.

There can be no forgiveness where perpetrators, whether individuals or collectives, lack the courage to disarm themselves in front of the victims. This is a painful and demanding act, and yet it is only one side of the process. Another painful *Entblössung* is required of the victims. As they are faced with the "disarming" confession of the perpetrator, they too are brought back to the origin of their hurt. It is by no means easy to allow this source of shameful humiliation to be reopened. Indeed, it may well be more difficult to acknowledge the evil one has suffered than the evil one has done. The experience of brutally enforced powerlessness impairs our self-worth more deeply than the experience of falsely gained superiority.

This is highlighted by a comment by the Jewish writer David Grossmann on the fiftieth anniversary of the liberation of Auschwitz, 27 January 1995, in the German weekly newspaper *Die Zeit*: "Whenever I think back on the Holocaust the predominant feeling continues to be that of hurt. It is not anger or lust for revenge, it is not hatred, but a bitter, inconsolable hurt that such things were done to human beings." Hurt is an impairment of the core of our personhood and leads to an almost cosmic sense of insecurity. Consequently, there are many good reasons why victims want to avoid returning to the depth of their traumatic hurt. It seems easier to hide behind barricades of repression, anger and self-righteousness.

So it is by no means self-evident that any sincere plea for forgiveness should automatically be met by an immediate and positive response. There is a moment of *Entblössung* and disarmament on the victims' side which must be taken very seriously indeed. But when forgiving does happen it leads to the profound recognition that the pain of the other is also my pain. There is a mutuality of defenceless openness which enables each side to recognize in the other a human being in need of help. Forgiving is more than an encounter; it is an exchange of pain. The result is a deepened understanding of the other and of oneself.

By entering into the pain of the other an overwhelming liberation takes place. It is hardly surprising, therefore, that acts of genuine forgiveness lead to tearful embraces. When Esau and Jacob met after twenty years of enmity they embraced each other and wept (Gen. 33:4). When Joseph forgave his brothers, they wept (Gen. 50:17). The woman who knelt at the feet of Jesus wet them with her tears (Luke 7:38). When Peter realized how he had betrayed Jesus he went away and wept bitterly (Matt. 26:75). These biblical accounts indicate that forgiveness implies a profound turmoil of emotions, a shaking-up of deep-seated bitterness and shame, but also the discovery of a kind of joy never known before.

This can be illustrated by what happened to a group of Germans and Belorussians in 1994. A group of old men who had fought in Hitler's army in Belorussia during the second world war decided to return to that country fifty years later and to do something productive. So they built a home for children affected by the Chernobyl nuclear disaster. At the end of their stay, which lasted several weeks, they went to see the war memorial at Chatyn. Upon their return they sat together with their Belorussian hosts. None of them will ever forget what happened that night.

> The toasts had all been very personal. Then one man from [the German] group got up and struggled to say a few words. I noticed that he was still overcome by what he had seen in Chatyn. He talked of his own history, that he had been in the war, that he had been in a Russian prisoner-of-war-camp, and then he stopped, and we all sensed that the moment had come at which one could not simply go on remembering — something redeeming might happen. And it happened.
>
> The man excused himself. He said that he felt deeply sorry for what he had done as a person, and for what the Germans had done in Russia. And then he tried to say that this must never happen again, but his voice broke. He had to sit down because he wept so hard. Around him there were young people. They were overcome and they too were weeping. Then an old woman got up, went over to that man — she was a Belorussian woman — and took him into her arms and kissed him. [3]

Under "normal" circumstances this old German might well have carried his guilt unacknowledged to his grave. In fact this is what happens in the majority of similar cases, not just among German soldiers. But he allowed himself to be swept beyond the confines of the ordinary by facing the past, exemplified by the Chatyn memorial, and somehow he gathered the courage completely to disarm himself. Similarly, the old Belorussian woman would never have thought it possible to embrace a former German soldier. His tears and her kiss were the seals of forgiveness and at the same time a sign of the power that transcends the accustomed patterns of hatred, distrust and prejudice, a power that overcomes deep-seated barriers and lays the ground for new trust.

So at the heart of pain there is a moment of grace. To this the gospel testifies: "The light shines *in* the darkness" (John 1:5). The gospel does not say that the light dispels the darkness; it simply affirms that it shines out in the midst of it and that it becomes visible for those who dare to enter into it.

The story of the former German soldier and the Belorussian woman helps us to see that the process of forgiveness is not only a liberation from bondage. It also releases a corrective and restoring power. It *corrects* the distortion which an act of evil establishes between two people or groups — the distortion of stolen power and enforced impotence. At the same time such correction *restores* the dignity of both sides. They recover their true height, as it were. While the perpetrator renounces his or her false aggrandizement, the victim rises from his or her induced humiliation. This mutual correction enables both partners to meet each other face to face. The restoration of dignified and equal humanity is a moment of grace, of overwhelming beauty and bliss. This is why Jesus insists that there is more joy in heaven over one sinner who truly repents than over ninety-nine righteous persons who think that they need no repentance (Luke 15:7).

The small incident in Belorussia enables us to see some additional aspects involved in processes of forgiveness. Let me mention five.

1. *To make amends without confession is not sufficient.* To be sure, it was a brave initiative of the old Germans to build this children's home, and there was considerable appreciation for it on the side of the Belorussian people, so that during the construction a tent of trust evolved which helped to bring the two parties closer together. This might have led the former German soldiers to think that their humanitarian initiative was in itself a clear sign of good will and a sufficient symbol of restitution. But to have hidden their confession behind this facade would have been a subtle form of denial. The months-long work of building the home was a useful act, but as an *act of repentance* it gained its importance only in and through the tearful confession of the old soldier.

This helps to explain why the enormous restitution payments by German governments since the second world war have never achieved their full healing dimension: it is because they were not accompanied by acts of acknowledgment which were experienced as convincing on the side of the victim.

2. When the old Germans came back, they did not try to repair some damage done during the war but directed their initiative towards the needs of the coming generation. This exemplifies that acts of restitution need not — and indeed cannot — re-establish the situation as it existed before the evil act was done. The word "restitution" suggests that it possible to "repair" the past. But that is an illusion. In a strict sense it is not possible to restitute the status quo ante. What is possible, however, are efforts to inaugurate better conditions. *The emphasis must not be on repairing the past, but on preparing a better way forward.*

3. Those old Germans had been young soldiers when they were marched off to Belorussia. They could have denied any responsibility for what they had done or were ordered to do. This is what soldiers have done at all times. They could have numbed themselves so as not to admit any ethical doubts about their atrocious deeds. [4] Indeed, it is likely that many of them had tried to repress their memories for many years. But as they reached the end of their lives they were honest enough to face the sins of their youth.

Fifty years is a long time — too long for many victims. But it enables us to see the gravity of shame and the power of numbing that frustrate all easy and quick "solutions". There is no automatism in "putting things right again". The pain of guilt takes time to form itself until it cannot be suppressed any longer.

It is a grave error to say, as people often do, that time heals all wounds. But we do well to bear in mind that it is never too late to turn around and to account for past deeds. Time does not undo evil, but carries the impact and weight of past deeds along. Yet *time also upholds the option to face our evil deeds rather than to keep denying them until our last breath.*

4. Only one of the old Germans in this story broke down. But his words and tears redeemed the entire group. *There is something profoundly vicarious in a genuine act of confession; for it brings the unspoken — and unspeakable — words of all into the open.* Often it is

enough for one person to be there to find the necessary words, or to try to utter them. But it takes at least one to break the chain of denial, to disarm himself or herself and to enter nakedly into the pain. The vicarious leader, the one who is strong enough to break down, is a very rare person, but on such human beings depends whether history can turn towards healing past affliction or whether it will simply continue its fateful, repetitive course.

5. The story mentions some young people who were overcome by the tears of the old German and who wept too. Were they simply carried away by the emotional impact of the old man's tale? It is probably more accurate to say that they were overcome by the presence of the healing which connects the generations whenever true repentance is felt.

These young people were born long after the war. They had no direct involvement in it, yet the sufferings of their parents and grandparents constitute their heritage. They are part and parcel of that bitter bondage because they are victims of their parents' victimization. Consequently, they need to be set free too. They also wait for acts of total disclosure to break the chains of mistrust, cynicism and revenge that lock generations together. They too are waiting for the demons of the past to be cast out.

So *it is wrong to say that only the victims can forgive*. The victims have their history too, and they make history. Their pain influences the coming generations, especially if it is never openly addressed.[5] It is essential to take the intergenerational impact of suffering into account and to involve the coming generations in the processes of forgiveness. For genuine forgiveness is about unburdening the past in order to inaugurate less painful relationships in the future. Forgiveness is an intergenerational challenge and a precious opportunity to build new bonds in the place of bitter bondage.

NOTES

[1] Hannah Arendt, *The Human Condition*, Chicago: University of Chicago Press, 1958, p.240.

[2] See Robert J. Lifton, *The Broken Connection: On Death and the Continuity of Life*, New York, Basic Books, 1972.

[3] D. Weber, "Ich musste den Weg noch einmal zurückgehen" (I had to take the way back once again), *Publik-Forum* no. 24, 20 Dec. 1994, p.48.

[4] This is what was done by the German physicians whose interviews with psychologist Robert J. Lifton thirty years after the war are the basis of his book *The Nazi Doctors: Medical Killing and the Psychology of Genocide*, New York, Basic Books, 1986.

[5] This is brought out with haunting clarity by Helen Epstein, *Children of the Holocaust*, New York, G.P. Putnam, 1979.

5. The Go-Between Factor

Former German Chancellor Helmut Schmidt recounts a story from the first visit of Soviet leader Leonid Brezhnev to Bonn in May 1973. On one evening there was a meeting in the residence of Willy Brandt, who was then chancellor. The atmosphere was cordial until Brezhnev began to recall in great detail some of the atrocities committed by Nazi troops in Russia. Everyone was listening with a mixture of respect and dread, because it was obvious that the Soviet leader had to free himself of these oppressive memories. His words had to be understood as an indication of what it had cost the Russians to come to the capital of Germany — the heart of what had been their most bitter enemy.

Brezhnev spoke for some twenty minutes. Then Schmidt, who was minister of defence at the time, responded by telling his own story, for he had been one of the German soldiers stationed in Russia. He spoke of the schizophrenic situation of German soldiers who did not adhere to the Nazi ideology but had been educated to be patriots and thus felt bound to defend their country. In recalling this encounter nearly 15 years later, Schmidt comes to a revealing conclusion: he writes that this "exchange of bitter memories greatly contributed to the mutual respect" that existed between him and Brezhnev despite the fact that the two found themselves in opposite camps from that evening up to the end of their terms of office. [1]

Schmidt observes that it was the presence of Willy Brandt that made this disarming encounter possible. Brandt was the trusted friend of both. He had set a powerful precedent of repentance when he knelt down in front of the memorial of the Warsaw uprising. That sudden gesture had been an act of surrender to the shame Germany felt with regard to the Polish people and the Jews among them. Having been a resistance fighter against Hitler, exiled in Norway, Brandt could easily have exonerated himself from any guilt of the Nazi régime. But he *vicariously* identified himself completely with the history of his nation, and so he took it upon himself to humble himself so that the victims' honour should be restored.

The presence of this man and the privacy of the evening meal made it easier for Brezhnev and Schmidt to reveal their traumatic memories. What was it that the presence of Brandt added to the courage and honesty of Brezhnev and Schmidt? It must be called the element of trust. It is trust that accompanies any genuine account of shame and hurt. Where does it come from?

When we study processes of forgiveness, we discover that often a *mediating agent* has been in place — a therapist, a friend, a neighbour, someone sufficiently trusted by both conflicting partners to release the spark of confidence needed to initiate the process of *Entblössung*. In social and political conflicts it has proved indispensable to seek the help of such mediating agents. The two sides who are in conflict need a go-between who is sufficiently trusted to build a bridge between them. Former US President Jimmy Carter has often served in this capacity. Obviously, this go-between can only be an initial spark to light the fire of encounter and to enable both sides to meet each other face to face.

It is not always possible or indeed necessary to bring in a mediating agent. As we have seen from the story of the old German and the Belorussian woman, it can be a visit to a memorial or some other deep experience which makes the barricades of fear and suspicion come down. It may also be the sheer weight of guilt or the unbearable burden of alienation which causes human beings to throw their heart over the fence, as it were, and to plead for pardon.

In his famous book *I and Thou* Martin Buber shows that wherever there is a genuine encounter between persons something new emerges, an energy which neither possesses within himself or herself or in isolation from the other, but which originates in their coming together. Whenever two human beings reveal themselves to each other, an "energy-field" is established between them which transcends their individual strengths. In religious discourse this surprising energy is referred to as God's Spirit. Since it appears so amazing and new, people talk about it as a charismatic inspiration or an illumination from outside. This enables them to describe processes they would normally have considered impossible.

But it is not necessary to use religious language to understand processes of forgiveness, though it is evident that the transforming power of a deep faith commitment can and does enable people to transcend defensiveness, hatred and fear. Hannah Arendt has gone so far as to argue that Jesus was "the discoverer of the role of forgiveness in the realm of human affairs", but she goes on to say that its religious context should not prevent us from taking this discovery seriously in a strictly secular sense. She says Jesus emphasized that the human capacity to forgive should not be reduced to the divine mercy, but should be recognized as a genuinely human capacity.[2] We may say that it was Jesus' "God-centredness" (to use Gil Bailie's term) which enabled him to live out the paramount importance of forgiveness. He possessed within himself the "third factor" which transformed him into the pivotal agent of redemption. This is reflected in the way all four gospels depict his baptism as the transforming moment at which God's Spirit took possession of him (Matt. 3:16f.; Mark 1:10f.; Luke 3:21f.; John 1:32). But this "third factor" or "go-between" element can also be found among persons who do not consider themselves religious. We can call this energy the *power of contingency*.

As we have said, human beings are not simply the products of the formative impulses of their past. They are more than the sum total of the physical, emotional, historical and social influences to which they have been exposed. As they interact with others there is always something more, something surprising, unexpected, unaccountable. This element of contingency turns human beings into subjects of their destiny and constitutes their uniqueness. The capacity to say "I" and to recognize in others the "Thou" is intimately linked to the element of freedom. It is important for us to become more actively aware of these contingent powers and to enable each other to trust in them.

This reference to our contingent human capacities should not be seen as contradicting what Luther and others said about the "unfree will". Luther's insistence on sin as an existential fate should not be read as an ontological verdict, but as a profound insight into the pervasive reality of violence and the contagious mechanism of sacrificial "release" which it keeps producing. The argument here is that the historic reality of Jesus is a significant indication of the presence of the transcending energy within human history.

As we reflect on the human capacity to arrive at contingent solutions we come across a related phenomenon. Contingency and imagination are closely interrelated. The "go-between" agents appear as those with unexpected and imaginative proposals. They see images of solutions which the conflicting partners are unable or unwilling to grasp. This capacity to imagine unprecedented options is central to processes of forgiveness. While the double bondage of shame and hurt blocks the mind, forgiveness releases new images of togetherness. While anger and defensiveness cast the shadow of doubt over each fresh suggestion, the energy of mutual disclosure expresses itself in new avenues towards the future. Such images of fresh beginnings are the fruit of liberation from the bondage of past hurts.

NOTES

[1] Helmut Schmidt, *Menschen und Mächte*, Berlin, Siedler Verlag, 1987, p.20.
[2] *The Human Condition*, pp.238ff.

6. The Art of Re-Membering

We have emphasized that forgiveness is a process by which people are healed from the bondage that keeps them locked to some past evil, so that they can inaugurate more trusting relationships leading towards a less hurtful future. This is a point worth repeating because much of the widespread disregard for forgiveness has to do with the impression that it is concerned only with overcoming past grievances or, more cheaply still, with *forgetting* past injustices. Thus people often say "forgive and forget" as though the two were synonymous. "Let bygones be bygone! Let's get on with it!" Against this is the Jewish proverb "Forgetting prolongs captivity. Remembering is the secret of redemption." In this chapter, therefore, we shall look at the relationship between forgiving and remembering.

We have pointed out that forgiveness leads those involved through the narrow gates of pain into the blissful discovery of mutual liberation. A healing takes place which sets the stage for renewed relationships built on trust and gratitude.

This does not mean that the hurtful past is simply forgotten. It remains part of one's past and cannot simply vanish in a pit of oblivion. But the sting of festering bitterness has left and something supremely precious has taken its place — a commitment to try again, a readiness to start afresh. Only those things that no longer hurt can safely be forgotten. They disappear like wounds that have healed without a scar. But most wounds do leave scars, and they are bound to ache at times. Yet, such scars will not be used to remind the other side of past grievances, because they have become part of a shared past.

This leads to another precious phenomenon: anyone who has gone through the disarming process of acknowledgment and experienced the utter joy of deliverance emerges with a new and profound awareness of the human condition. Those who have seen the light shining in the darkness develop a sensitivity to the profound similarity of human beings and the dreadful presence of fury within every human heart. Genuine forgiveness leaves an imprint of humility on all who have experienced it. They have come face to face with the awesome weight of violence in the caverns of each human soul and have sensed the deep need of every human being for something that can only be called redemption.

Words like awareness, understanding, sensitivity and empathy point at an attitude to human affairs that goes beyond all attempts to forget or suppress past hurts or to harbour animosities and thoughts of vengeance. It is this kind of remembering of which the Jewish proverb speaks — a "re-membering" in the original sense of bringing together the members and pieces of something that was once complete, a joining together of what has been severed, a making whole of that which is broken, a restoring of the distorted.

It is relevant in this context to remember a leitmotif that runs through the history of Israel as reflected in the Hebrew Bible: the consistent references by prophets and wisdom teachers to Israel's experiences in Egypt. "You shall not oppress a resident alien, you know the heart of an alien, for you were aliens in the land of Egypt" (Ex. 23:9). You know "how it feels" — and to know how it feels is the beginning of wisdom. Thus the admonition "Remember Egypt!" leads to laws that focus on the protection of the aliens, the weak and powerless.

How sharply this contrasts with the battle-cry still sometimes heard in the United States: "Remember Pearl Harbor!" More than 50 years later, this slogan calls to mind the devastating surprise attack by Japanese bombers on the US warships docked in that Hawaiian port in 1941. "The Japanese attack remained the arch-symbol of the stab in the back," remarks J. W. Dower.[1] Hence the slogan "Remember Pearl Harbor!" is a call to vigilance and suspicion with regard to the Japanese and continues to stand in the way of a thorough reconciliation between these two nations. Pearl Harbor and Hiroshima are set one against the other, not as symbols of how it feels to be the alien, but as symbols of how to be on guard against the alien. So not every kind of remembering can be called redemptive.[2] In fact, memories that are used to maintain and solidify stereotypes of the enemy help to prolong captivity and make forgiveness even more difficult.

Forgiveness is concerned with a certain healing of memories. It cleanses them of their bitter and aggressive components and focuses on the innermost likeness of the human quest. It has seen the "I" in the "Thou", even the enemy, and has learned to tremble at the massive violence brooding in the depths of human consciousness.

Reflecting on the relationship between forgiving and remembering sheds new light on forgiveness as a process which liberates people from the chains of past guilt and hurt in order to inaugurate more constructive ways towards the future. To explain this, let me cite Hannah Arendt again. She speaks not only about the human capacity to forgive as a means of breaking the chains that lock people to the past, but also about the human capacity to make and keep promises as a way to make the future safe. She argues that this is the only means by which free persons can agree to create "islands of predictability" and "guideposts of reliability" in the "ocean of uncertainty" caused by "the darkness of the human heart" and the fundamental unaccountability of human nature without succumbing to authoritarian rule and subsequent loss of freedom.[3]

Arendt does not connect these two capacities, although it would appear to be the logical conclusion of her reasoning. For is the bottomless unaccountability of the human heart not deeply conditioned by the unresolved and unredeemed feelings of guilt and hurt that haunt the human psyche? Brooding violence is among the reasons why humans beings are unreliable. Psychological research has made abundantly clear the profound impact of unresolved and traumatic experiences on the ability of human beings to act responsibly. Hence a great deal of what makes us fearful of the future lies in the past — specifically in unresolved problems and feelings that have not come to rest but keep haunting our future and obscure our vision of the tasks ahead.

Therefore, it seems to me that the capacity to ask for and to grant forgiveness and the capacity to make and keep promises must be closely related. This is apparent in the realm of politics, to which we turn in the next part of this book. It is also evident in our personal affairs, as the example of the traditional wedding ceremony shows. Before the bride and groom make their marriage vows, there is a reference to the past. In the archaic language of the ancient formula, the officiating minister says, "If anyone can show cause why these two should not be united in holy matrimony, let him speak now or forever hold his peace." This means that the past must be clear if the future of the two persons is to stand on solid ground.

It goes without saying that this can never be attained completely. Insecurity remains which can never be fully accounted for. But one thing is obvious: the ancient marriage liturgy elucidates how important it is to clear the past (as much as possible) in order to secure a somewhat safe road towards the future. The most haunting enemies of a reliable and peaceful future are the unresolved and dis-membered legacies of the past.

NOTES

[1] Quoted in Shriver, *An Ethic for Enemies*, p.123.
[2] "Remember Pearl Harbor" must be regarded as an element which added to the massive denial of the unprecedented use of the atomic bomb by the US in August 1945 against the Japanese cities of Hiroshima and Nagasaki; cf. Robert J. Lifton and Greg Mitchell, *Hiroshima in America: Fifty Years of Denial*, New York, Grosset, 1995.
[3] Hannah Arendt, *The Human Condition*, pp.244f.

Part Two

Deep Remembering
in Politics
and Public Life

7. *Forgiveness and Politics*

Is forgiveness an element in politics? Can it be one of the principles that influence how nations order their interests and conflicts? The preceding chapters have already hinted that forgiveness can and must be brought into the political arena.

As a matter of fact, recent books by Brian Frost and Donald Shriver have argued that it is already there.[1] Frost provides an overview of approaches to forgiveness in all parts of the world, while Shriver offers an in-depth study of elements of forgiveness in US policies towards Germany and Japan after the second world war, as well as in internal relationships between white Americans and African-Americans.

But these are lonely and almost eccentric views. The overwhelming majority of politicians would say that it would of course be nice if forgiveness played a larger role in political affairs, but alas, the brutal facts of life require other methods. People and nations, being what they are, will be moved only by pressure, threat and retaliation.

It goes without saying that no Christian church can ever want to renew the mediaeval claim to possess the "keys to the kingdom of heaven". Not only has Christianity ceased to be a centralized political power, but more importantly, most people could not care less about this sort of kingdom. And yet, as we have seen, forgiveness is central to the lives of people, just as guilt and hurt are immediate realities of individual and collective human existence. Hence we must assume that political affairs are profoundly influenced by these realities, and that it is of paramount importance to understand these dynamics as precisely as possible if we are ever to leave behind the vicious cycle of revenge and retaliation.

To make the bridge from theological to political considerations, we may begin by looking at Dietrich Bonhoeffer's view on this question:

> The church experiences in faith the forgiveness of all her sins and a new beginning through grace. For the nations there is only a healing of the wound, a cicatrization of guilt, in the return to order, to justice, to peace and to the granting of free passage to the church's proclamation of Jesus Christ. [2]

Bonhoeffer essentially regards forgiveness as a theological category. God alone can grant a complete break with guilt, and only committed Christians and the true church are capable of experiencing this. God is the forgiving agent; the faithful can only receive it.

As for the guilt between nations, Bonhoeffer agrees that processes of scarring over can and do occur whenever violence is transformed into law and war into peace, and such processes may be called "forgiveness within history" (*innergeschichtliche Vergebung*). But he goes on to say that this type of forgiveness can be but a shadowy reflection of the "real forgiveness" which comes from God.

For two reasons Bonhoeffer's approach is unconvincing. The first is his outspoken "verticalist" and theocentric perspective. If God is the sole subject of forgiveness, the sinner can only be seen as the receiver and the sinned-against does not come into focus at all. This results in a rather abstract understanding of the historical relevance of forgiveness. It is presented as a sudden break whose consequences remain obscure.

Second, Bonhoeffer argues for processes of healing in time without reflecting on the subjects of this healing. But there are no trans-human self-healing processes in history. The issue of how agents of violence can become agents of law and victims of war turn into subjects of peace Bonhoeffer does not address. What is required to bring about such profound changes in the consciousness of collectives and to empower people to transcend their condition? Bonhoeffer's verticalist concept of forgiveness prevents him from posing such concrete historical questions.

The approach offered by Hannah Arendt seems more helpful. She notes that whereas the human capacity to make and keep promises has become an important instrument of politics, the capacity to ask for and to grant forgiveness has yet to find its way into this arena. In the previous chapter I suggested that there is a link between these two capacities. The reliability of treaties is directly correlated to the seriousness with which people try to clear up their past. What we might call the "covenanting principle" and the "forgiveness concept" are thus intimately related. If politics is the "art of the possible", what is possible depends largely on the availability of various options, and these are directly shaped by what we have called the "art of remembering".

It is doubtful that economic concerns are in fact the prime movers in the realm of politics. The values and options that guide economics are intimately linked to the fabric of general cultural values, which are in turn deeply influenced by the past. Our past is thus a far more powerful agent in the formation of our personal and collective options than is commonly acknowledged. And much of its power depends on the fact that it is exercised in unconscious forms and shapes.

The official reading of our national past which we want passed on to our children is a highly selective one, influenced by subtle decisions about what does and does not suit our national self-esteem, sense of identity, "grandeur" and "mission". Only a fraction of this is conveyed in history classes in the schools. Many other "teachers of history" contribute to our collective self-awareness in much more subliminal ways. Some of these are part of our symbolic narrative — the national anthem, the flag, national holidays, songs, speeches. Memories are enshrined in mythic accounts, in festivals, dances, poems and plays. This official narrative is fed in many ways. War memorials, for instance, recall the sacrifices of our own soldiers and the heroism of our leaders.

The traumas and triumphs of our past inform our identity and shape the way we perceive our mission for the future. Hence it is fair to say that a nation's conscious and unconscious memories are the raw materials of its policies and politics. It can, therefore, be assumed that a direct relationship exists between the reliability of a collective and its accountability for its past. A nation that is clear and honest about its history can be a trusted covenant partner for its neighbours. Such a healthy "economy of memories" is the founding principle of any form of dependable and authentic politics.

NOTES

[1] See Brian Frost, *The Politics of Peace*, London, Darton, Longman & Todd, 1991; Donald W. Shriver, *An Ethic for Enemies: Forgiveness in Politics*.

[2] D. Bonhoeffer, *Ethics*, New York, Macmillan, 1965, p.117.

8. Towards Deep Remembering

In 1989 the Serbian leader Slobodan Milosevic headed the celebrations commemorating the 600th anniversary of the Battle of the Kosovo in 1389, when the Serbs had fought against the troops of the emerging Ottoman Empire and lost. Their defeat sealed hundreds of years of subordination to the sultans of Constantinople. Remembering this battle became the interpretative key for the formation of the identity of the Serbian people. They had fought to defend the values of Christian Europe against the Turkish infidels. Yet since this sacrifice had never been appreciated, Serbs came to see themselves as the heroic victims. To use the expression coined by psychologist and peace researcher Vamik Volkan, this is the "chosen trauma" of the Serbian nation. It became the key to reading their history, enabling them not only to create and nurture their own self-image but also to identify their enemies and to generate patterns of suspicion and hatred.

It is no exaggeration to link this process of selective remembering to the murderous orgies of aggression and ethnic cleansing which followed the outbreak of war in the former Yugoslavia not long after these celebrations. Six hundred years had not sufficed to heal the traumatic wounds caused by that defeat on the Kosovo. Time and again this date had been used to open up the wounds, to renew the hurt and to nourish the lust for revenge. At the anniversary celebrations in 1989, Milosevic and other former communists drew on the historic national trauma of the Serbian people to reassert their own power in the aftermath of the ideological vacuum which was left by the demise of communism.

While this recent example is fresh in our memories, I do not cite it here to single out the Serbian nation. What their leaders have done is done everywhere else as well. Hitler's ideology was also based on a highly selective interpretation of history. For example, the "shame of Versailles" was one of the interpretative tools used by the Nazi party to create a version of the first world war that justified their nationalistic policies. Other examples from other peoples' histories could as easily be added. The point is that the amount of historical selectivity corresponds directly to the degree of chauvinism and nationalism. Claims to present greatness are related to glorious achievements in the past, and claims of revenge are justified by experiences of victimization long ago. All constructs of national pride and messianism are constantly "verified" by reference to the past. Similar concepts about neighbouring peoples are shaped by interpretative patterns derived from selective readings of their past. This is the reservoir that feeds enemy images and stereotypes.

As long as these collective identities are clearly separated from each other geographically, the conflictive potential of these images may remain relatively small, provided that no one is deriving expansionist policies from a perception of "national mission". This explains, for instance, why the impression that the Spanish or the Dutch have of the self-perception of the Swedish nation is quite different from that of the Finnish people, who have repeatedly been the victims of Swedish expansionism. Wherever the "memory-fields" of different peoples overlap and there are no clearly defined boundaries, clashes of identities can be expected; and these will lead to emphasizing differences rather than commonalities. The neighbours will and must be seen as the enemies.

Such destructive dynamics can be observed very clearly in Ireland or in certain parts of the former Yugoslavia. While foreigners will be unable to see any difference between an Irish Protestant and Catholic, or between a Serb, a Croat and a Bosnian, the insider will claim to know exactly who belongs to which group.

But what does this have to do with forgiveness? What we have called "selective remembering" is a way of rereading history that looks at national victories without counting the damage done to others, that is, without contemplating the guilt involved. It considers defeats solely in terms of unjust victimization, thereby laying the blame entirely on the others. Selective remembering necessarily produces ideologies of denial and suppression. It needs to demonize the other in order to preserve its own purity and sense of mission, thus leading to cultures of revenge and policies of retaliation. Often, selective remembering will be related closely to racism, helping to turn shades of skin colour into ontological differences. [1] Selective remembering ultimately leads to the dehumanization of the fellow human being across the border.

Processes of forgiveness, by contrast, start by taking into account the victims of each victory. Here the concern is for the ones who always have to pay the bill. Forgiveness looks at history from the underside. It uncovers denial and oppression. Behind the great conqueror it sees the soldiers who were slain; behind the names of the mighty it remembers the names of those who do not count.

Forgiveness knows that victims are the same everywhere. So it approaches history in a more inclusive way. It transcends the borderlines and recognizes that human beings are essentially the same here and there and everywhere.

This is what we call "deep remembering". It is grateful for genuine greatness, but it does not shun guilt and suppression. It rejoices in human inventiveness and ingenuity, but it also shares in the many forms of suffering. It regards the wealth of peoples, races and cultures as transient constellations in the evolution of the human race, to be cherished for the beautiful variety they have in store, but never to be idolized or absolutized.

Deep remembering is about transforming the art of the possible. It makes the possible possible.

NOTE

[1] Shriver makes this point very convincingly, showing the clearly racist connotations of the enmity between the US and Japan. Obviously, the same holds true in the internal relationships between white Americans and those of African origin; cf. *An Ethic for Enemies*, pp.121ff.

9. Collective Memories

Any marriage counsellor knows that it is impossible to make a neat distinction between the "guilty" and the "innocent" party in a divorce. The subtle interplay of various layers of dependencies, wounds and injustices between husband and wife makes it very difficult to determine why a marriage has failed. A counsellor will often be able to unearth profound formative experiences from early childhood, deep impulses and sometimes traumatic wounds that have left a lasting impact, perhaps casting the "guilty" partner in a light in which he or she appears as the victim of earlier injustices.

Similarly, when we talk about how groups of people, ethnic entities or entire nations deal with their memories and relate to each other, we need to take account of a certain fuzziness. Collectives are necessarily open-ended. There are always some who do not fit in or who move beyond the accustomed boundaries. Over the course of time ethnic groups have again and again melted into each other, making the very idea of "ethnic purity" a fiction. This is why the Nazis' efforts to construct and protect the pure Aryan race were not only accompanied by unspeakable atrocities but also utterly stupid. This also explains why the political programme of the National Party of South Africa to use racial criteria for the construction of apartheid and "separate development" could not be sustained, despite tremendous brutality. Furthermore, it underlines why all attempts at "ethnic cleansing" will be in vain. The amount of brutality needed to attempt the realization of a fiction only underscores the foolishness of such endeavours.

The idea of the nation-state on which the international political system is based has within it a great deal of artificiality. Modern nation-states are in fact little more than legal and administrative units, yet their political systems of governance constantly try to elicit feelings of belonging and support that transcend the mere constitutional requirements. In this context politics is deeply dependent on people's memories and is always trying to use them for particular ends.

To be sure, as long as nation-states are the prime agents of political decision-making, their political leadership will need to work towards some general sense of cohesion to accommodate divergent memories and loyalties. In this limited sense one may speak of "healthy patriotism". In other words, every nation-state — and within its boundaries every region, town and village — will to some degree be involved in the "economy of memories", that is, a constant process of appropriating and transforming the past.

When we talk about "deep remembering", we need to look at how peoples face up to their deep-seated memories of guilt and hurt. This is very complex, since feelings of culpability and suffering overlap each other.

From the outside, Germany after the second world war might seem to be a simple and clear-cut example. The war itself was an obvious case of aggression, and the destruction of European Jews and other minorities — the Sinti and Roma, political or religiously motivated opponents, homosexual people — was a direct result of the Nazi ideology. And there is no doubt that one finds Germans who fully accept the legacy of the Nazi period — the "history of shame" (*Wirkungsgeschichte der Scham*). But other Germans still prefer to deny their full share in the shame of our history. To generalize and dissipate the burden of shame they compare what the Nazis did with the crimes of Stalin and others.

Still others remember the loss of their loved ones, the destruction of their homes in the bombed-out cities, the agonies of trekking towards the West under horrible conditions, the violence endured at the hands of the advancing Russian army. Remember that more than 12 million Germans had to flee their homes to make a living in some distant part of Germany which they had great difficulty recognizing as part of their "fatherland". These refugees will not so much identify with the crimes of the Nazi times as with the suffering they had to endure. Their hurt overshadows their sense of sharing in the guilt and shame. Some of them will argue that by their sufferings they have atoned for the crimes of the Nazis and stand acquitted.

Another group, especially those who were subjected to forty years of communist rule in the former German Democratic Republic, will remember only the price they had to pay for the defeat of Nazi Germany. They have ample reason to envy those fellow-Germans who happened to live in the Western regions, who survived the war relatively unscathed and thereafter, through the Western alliance, enjoyed far better opportunities to prosper and flourish, even though their involvement in the nation's historic guilt was no less grave.

The point is that even in a situation which seems objectively clear, the emotional receptions can be very complex. This poses grave problems for those in leadership positions. They are faced with the question of how to administer such complex and divergent memories within the emotional household of one nation. It is easy to see why the German nation should be so confused and insecure about itself and thus appear to its neighbours as a confusing and even irritating partner.

Other nations and situations could be cited to underline the same point. To put it in general terms: the need to work on the formation of a collective identity constitutes a significant stress. The collective will be able to bear this stress only up to a certain point, and this "carrying capacity" will vary according to other stress-factors already at work. The pressure of collective identity-formation can only be internalized to a certain degree. If it goes beyond manageable limits, strategies will appear by which it is projected onto some internal subgroup that is somehow considered aberrant or some outside collective that provides a "reason" for violent attack. Either way, the need to stabilize the internal membership results in strategies of dis-memberment or the production of enmity. The greater the need of the political estab-lishment to dissipate internal dissatisfaction and to stabilize the collective, the more violent will be the scapegoating and aggressive-ness towards outward "enemies".

The fact that one can cite countless examples of this mechanism does not take away from the fact that some nations, like mine, have tended to be more aggressive than others and that some nations, like the Finnish or the Irish, have been victimized more than others. A sweeping claim that all nations and groups find themselves in the same predicament as far as historical guilt and hurt are concerned would be incorrect. The scales are very unevenly distributed, and deep remembering must take that into account.

This means that political leaders are obliged to face up to their nation's own particular history of shame and hurt. If I may refer again to my own country, it has often been argued that the haunting persistence of memories of the Nazi period even fifty years after the second world war might be much less pervasive and painful if there had been a more decisive and unequivocal acknowledgment of that period by the first German governments after the war. Instead, there was during the early 1950s a massive process of defensiveness and denial which brought back into their earlier positions the overwhelming majority of the judiciary and professional personnel in schools and universities, which contributed to stabilizing those economic sectors which had been prominent under Hitler.

The German people are in no way exceptional in this tendency to deny the guilt-aspect of their past.[1] To admit heinous wrongs in the past is generally considered an act of weakness by which a nation gives away some of its bargaining-power. On the other hand, it is equally difficult for a people to admit grief about great injustices it has suffered without trying to transform this into policies of assertive self-defence. Each collective must face the need to engage in processes of acknowledging its particular history of wrongs and sufferings. This "economy of memories" should be regarded as a constitutive element of nation-building and corporate identity formation.

In European history two groups of people especially have been consistently subjected to the violent mechanism of scapegoating. One must mention the Jewish people first. Anti-semitism has been a constant ideological tool by which European — and Christian — societies have blamed this minority for various forms of internal stress, including plagues and natural disasters. The epitome of this scapegoating violence was of course the systematic destruction of the European Jews by Nazi Germany. A similar fate has befallen the Sinti and Roma, otherwise called "Gypsies". Their nomadic life has made them perfect targets of the "settled" communities.

In this context one may also think of the peoples whom Europeans encountered as they set about to colonize Africa, Asia and the Americas. These "savages" could be seen as noble or brutal according to needs the European peoples had to project at a given moment, but in either case they could be treated as a special kind of human being standing outside normal "civilized" culture. Most often they were described and treated as sub-human creatures, making them ideal targets of the violence that accumulated again and again within the established societies. And the difference of skin colour could be appealed to as proof of their "inhuman" nature and status. This explains why racism has become so pervasive a characteristic in the justification of all kinds of violent treatment, dispossession of lands and exploitation of resources.

Deep remembering is the attempt to unearth such hidden and shameful aspects of our past. It seeks to understand the urges and motives that guide our actions as individuals and collectives in unacknowledged and thus uncontrolled ways. What is most difficult to understand and to face is the violence that keeps accumulating within societies as a consequence of their need to cope with each other.

Do collectives need enemies and scapegoats in order constantly to re-establish their own cohesiveness? Is outward violence the price to be paid for the stress of group identity and inward solidarity? If no alternative can be found to this disastrous mechanism, then there is no end to strife, peace is no more than a breathing space between wars and all who fall outside the "normal" behavioural patterns can never feel safe. But it is possible to break through these patterns and to open up new avenues of understanding and cooperation. Let us briefly look at one historic example.

On 20 November 1977, President Anwar Sadat of Egypt appeared before the Knesset in Jerusalem and proposed a peaceful settlement. It was a stupendous move across the abyss of resentment, anger, suspicion and hatred that divided Israel from the Arab world. In his address to the Israeli government and parliament the Egyptian politician reminded his bitter enemies of their common heritage: "We all, Muslims, Christians and Jews, bow down before God... The teachings and commandments of God are messages of love, of sincerity, of security and peace." This reference to the common basis of the Abrahimitic faiths was an act of deep remembering. By moving beyond the standard ideological justifications of enmity between Muslims, Jews and Christians, it helped to dissolve the stereotypes with which the nations in the Middle East viewed each other and to rid the political agents of these countries of their accustomed projections and violent extrapolations.

Sadat's daring move resulted in a laborious process of reviewing and reorganizing the customary power-play among the political parties in that region. It contributed to the acknowledgment of their profound interdependence. "We do not want," Sadat declared, "that you or we should be locked into a circle of rockets ready to be aimed at each other, nor do we want to be encircled by grenades of anger and hatred."

Sadat's dramatic move was not immediately understood nor appreciated by people in all camps. Fellow Arabs bitterly attacked him as a traitor to their cause, and Egypt was isolated for many years. The peace process itself progressed very slowly indeed, and it needed the resolute support of President Carter to bring the Camp David negotiations to a successful conclusion. Sadat himself was assassinated by one of his own soldiers nearly four years after his visit to Jerusalem. Since he had taken away from the army the outward target of their aggressiveness, Sadat himself became scapegoat for their resentment. The violence which had lost its traditional target found a new one in him.

Two decades later, it is very clear that this daring leader set in motion a profound process of reshaping political power structures and social, economic and cultural relationships in the Middle East. To be sure, there continue to be setbacks and dangerous aberrations, such as the assassination of Israel's Prime Minister Yitzhak Rabin in November 1995. Nevertheless, it has become very difficult to imagine a return to the disastrous wars that locked Israel and its neighbours in a deadly embrace. A deeper awareness of their common interests and a greater sensitivity for their profound mutual dependence has grown up.

Psychologist and peace researcher Vamik D. Volkan argues that human beings develop several identities. Beyond their identity as individual persons, they also have an identity as members of a family or clan; and beyond these are corporate identities encompassing ethnic and national units. Volkan describes these more complex collective identities which cover an entire group or people as "canopies". Political leaders derive much of their influence from their ability to formulate and represent this collective identity. We referred above to the way President Milosevic provided a new sense of identity to the Serbian people after the collapse of communist Yugoslavia by evoking the memories of the Battle of the Kosovo. The case of Serbia helps us to see why collective and national identities must never become more than canopies, that is, flexible and adjustable structures providing some measure of protection, but nevertheless transient, not to be used as a fortress or encampment for their members. They can be strikingly beautiful, but they do not last forever.

When Sadat flew from Cairo to Jerusalem he left the Arab canopy. His reference to the one God who is at the heart of Muslims, Christians and Jews indicates that he was aware of a larger tent. As a fervent believer and mystic, he was conscious of an identity informed and constituted by faith, a canopy which overarches national and tribal tents and provides a sense of belonging that transcends historical identities.

Brian Frost notes: "Sadat went from Muslim and Christian shrines to Yad Vashem, the memorial to Jews who died in the Holocaust, walking barefoot through its rooms. He wrote in the visitors' book: 'Let us put an end to all the sufferings of the human race.'"[2] Here is an indication that Sadat moved under a canopy which was far greater than the Middle East tent or even the tent of the Abrahamitic religions. We might call it the "humanity canopy". Sadat had come to see that it is the human race as a whole which suffers in the seemingly endless flow of attack and counter-attack, offence and retaliation. In other words, in looking beyond the confines of tribal identities Sadat envisaged the fundamental common identity of all human beings. Unless *all* political parties understand the need to care about *all* human suffering there will be no end to regional and local violence.

Happily, suffering and hardship are not the only things all of humanity shares. In *Die Mappe meines Grossvaters*, the 19th-century German writer Adalbert Stifter remarks that the little baby in the crib and the fly that plays beside it in the sunshine are the last members of a long and unknown chain, but also the first of another that might perhaps be even longer and lesser known still. "Yet," Stifter insists, "it is a chain of relationship and love, and each individual stands in the middle of it." He goes on to speak about the care and love which constitutes the chain of generations. Little attention is devoted to this flow of self-giving care. The historians who take note only of the big events leave out the love and record the bloodshed:

> The endless stream of love which through the centuries has come down to us, through countless mothers, through brides, fathers, sisters and brothers and friends, this love alone is the rule, but recording it has been forgotten. The other, the hatred, is the exception, and it has been written up in thousands of books.

Stifter manages to look through the haze of a thousand books on hatred to identify the "stream of love" that sustains life from one generation to the next. This, he maintains, is the true raison d'être and generative principle of all life. And so Stifter discovers an identity that surpasses the tribal and national identity tents. It even transcends the humanity-canopy by including "the baby and the fly", pointing to the basic togetherness of all life forms on this planet.

There is an element of wisdom here that flows from the art of deep remembering. Stifter saw it, as did Sadat, and as have many others. This kind of wisdom results from a heightened awareness of the forces at work in every human being, of the kindness and violence, love and rage found in every human heart.

By underlining this in-built ambiguity within human beings I am trying to avert the misunderstanding that the reference to our basic humanity is unequivocal. "Deep remembering" does not mean trying to conceal the haunting tensions in the human heart. But it is convinced that by naming and acknowledging these tensions we humans can endeavour to re-member what is constantly being dis-membered, to put the missing pieces back into place, to unite what is being torn apart all the time. The fact is that we cannot be certain of ourselves. This is a deeply disquieting insight which must elicit from us lament, humility and prudence. Such self-critical awareness is at the root of wisdom. It can help to dissipate violence and can empower us to express our constructive strengths.

There is another helpful facet to this reference to our common humanity. Brazilian educator Paulo Freire once remarked that for the oppressed the image of the human is the oppressor. Why is this so? Oppressed people are captives of a mechanism that binds them to their oppressor in many subtle ways, not only economic but also emotional. In this structure of dependence the oppressed see themselves as "subhuman", which means that in order to be human they must become like the oppressor. Consequently, they see "justice" as a process of exchanging places. In other words, justice is understood within the mechanism of retaliation, without overcoming the structure of dependency.

In this context it is extremely important to provide a vision of the human that reaches beyond the immediate social structures. Thought-forms, stories, songs and rituals are needed which enable oppressed and dependent people to see themselves and their future in ways not determined by those who lord it over them. This involves acknowledgment, grieving and cleansing — essentially healing processes which modern societies tend to be unable to provide. On the whole, traditional cultures have maintained a greater sensitivity for such rituals.

Why have such 20th-century political leaders as Sadat, Rabin and Mahatma Gandhi been assassinated, not by their enemies, but by their own people?[3] The answer must be that they had come to a position of leadership because they had managed to encapsulate the corporate identity of their respective peoples. So in a way these peoples felt they owned their leaders. However, as soon as these leaders ventured beyond their ethnocentric identity-tents to suggest a wider agenda encompassing traditional enemies, they created a vacuum and were seen as traitors. Consequently, they attracted the violence that had lost its external target.

Aware of this dangerous mechanism, many political leaders remain the champions of their national or tribal cause. In their determination to stay in power they spend a great deal of energy in solidifying their partial identity-tent. They can hope to move beyond it safely only when they can be sure that a sizeable part of their electorate is prepared to accept a challenge to their accustomed self-understanding.

This explains why many political leaders are reluctant and half-hearted advocates of transnational organizations like the United Nations. They realize of course that most of the factors that shape the daily life of their citizens are influenced, indeed determined, by international forces. The two most obvious examples are in economics and the media, but this applies equally to the international character of scientific research, the arts and entertainment. At the same time, they must try to single out special interests of their electorate, sometimes against their better judgment, to safeguard their position of power. To do so they will sometimes risk conflict with other groups or nations or employ scapegoating strategies to direct latent social dissatisfaction and violence against minorities such as homosexuals or immigrants.

Observers of political conflict have suggested a more differentiated approach, involving the establishment of transnational structures of reconciliation beginning with persons below the highest leadership level. According to Joseph Montville:

> Senior political leaders in intense conflict situations... are generally emotionally deeply invested in their public image and therefore not susceptible to change...; they are also limited in their room to manoeuvre by the negative emotions of their constituencies... Intellectual and spiritual leaders from other sectors of a community or nation may have to undertake the moral responsibility, paving the way for politicians to "catch up" with and hopefully transform this fundamental leadership by others into official policy. These non-political leaders could be academics, clergy, business people, trade union officials, poets or playwrights. What makes them leaders is their courage, wisdom and capacity to show the way. [4]

This insight is elaborated in some detail by John P. Lederach. He criticizes the customary "top-level" approaches to peace which focus on political leaders and their diplomatic agencies and suggests the development of "middle-range approaches" which use persons placed at intermediary levels: community leaders, trusted intellectual or spiritual persons close enough to the grassroots and with access to the top leadership. "If mobilized strategically," Lederach points out, "middle-range actors could hold the key to the long-term sustainability of conflict transformation."

To spell out the requirements for long-term peaceful settlements Lederach uses the term "reconciliation":

> Reconciliation is a central component of dealing with contemporary conflict and reconstructing divided societies. Reconciliation is understood as a process of relationship-building. Thus, reconciliation is not exclusively relegated to the period of post-conflict restoration. Rather, reconciliation provides a focus and a locus appropriate to every aspect of peacebuilding and essential to the sustainability of peace. [5]

Lederach's "reconciliation" comes close to what we have called deep remembering. Various groups within any given society are capable of formulating insights, experiences and values that reach beyond the conflict and provide the basis for lasting peace. Remembering is thus a process which, by calling to mind the deepest convictions and possibilities of people, encourages them to heal forms of dis-memberment and to work for a united society. The art of remembering is not an exercise in looking backwards but an effort to transfigure past pains in order to construct vital and forward-looking societies.

To remember is thus much more than a process of the mind and emotions by which we look at our past. It is a way of re-living the anguish and bitterness of the past in order to arrive at a more profound awareness of the human condition. This enables us to link with other members of our immediate communities and to reach beyond them to the whole human race and to all forms of life on earth. The art of remembering is a constructive social exercise and thus constitutes the basis of sustainable politics.

NOTES

[1] We have already mentioned the processes of denial related to the US use of atomic bombs in Hiroshima and Nagasaki, as documented by Lifton and Mitchell, *Hiroshima in America*. Cf. also the official British avoidance of "moral responsibility to the Irish people for a centuries-old record of extraordinary violence and repression", which "has kept alive an Irish instinct toward violent defence"; Joseph V. Montville, "The Psychological Burdens of History", in Gregorian and Rasmusses, eds, *A Handbook for International Conflict Management and Resolution*, Washington, US Institute for Peace, 1995.

[2] Frost, *The Politics of Peace*, pp.48f.

[3] From an earlier time, Abraham Lincoln could also be included in this list, for he sought to transcend the barriers of hatred erected during the US Civil War. In his second inaugural address he invited his nation to accept the war as God's punishment for the evil of slavery. This reference to a greater design that far transcends the ethnocentrism of political parties and systems enabled Lincoln to envisage a politics of reconciliation and to declare, even before the war had ended, "With malice toward none, with charity for all, with firmness in the right as God gives us to see the right, let us strive to finish the work we are in, to bind up the nation's wounds, to care for him who shall have borne the battle and for his widow and his orphan, to do all which may achieve and cherish a just and lasting peace among ourselves and with all nations."

[4] Montville, *loc. cit.*

[5] John P. Lederach, *Building Peace: Sustainable Reconciliation in Divided Societies*, p.62.

10. How Can Collectives Communicate?

If guilt can be described as a breakdown in communication, forgiveness is about communicating with each other, about understanding the other side. But how do collectives communicate with each other? What kind of language, gestures, signs and symbols will the other side understand? How can collectives be helped to engage in the art of remembering?

We know from direct interpersonal communication how difficult it often is for us as individuals to find the appropriate words and to express our intentions and feelings with unequivocal clarity. How much more difficult it is to arrive at modes of communication which are meaningful to collectives such as ethnic groups and nations. Not only are they separated from each other by languages, but also by thick layers of cultural, religious and social differences. And it is all the more complicated when it comes to communicating guilt and hurt and arriving at meaningful expressions of reconciliation.

Obviously, collectives can communicate with each other only in *indirect* ways. Although their representatives will try to speak directly to their partners and opponents, they cannot and dare not do so for themselves alone but are requested to act on behalf of their nation or group. Besides, nations use sophisticated forms of diplomatic exchange, a complex representational system of communication which depends on various means of symbolic intercourse, including verbal and non-verbal codes, standard gestures and acts.

The flags and anthems that symbolize national identities illustrate this. To study the combination of colours and shapes of a flag or the text and melody of an anthem can reveal much about the founding myths of a national culture and the kind of images a nation has developed of itself — and sometimes of its messianic vocation. The "chosen traumas" and "chosen triumphs" that guide collectives in their way of reading history and asserting their present mission come out clearly in these texts.

State visits include rituals in which the sovereignty of the visited country is honoured. Among the traditional elements in these political "liturgies" are saluting the honour guard and laying down a wreath at a tomb of an unknown soldier or a comparable place which remembers the sacrifices of citizens for the integrity or grandeur of their nation. These and other examples underscore that we are surrounded by ethnocentric symbols and that there is an anxious interest in keeping the exchange between these symbolisms in a proper balance.

Kneeling in Warsaw and shaking hands in Bitburg

It would seem evident that these forms of indirect and symbolic communication are of little use in promoting deep remembering and forgiveness between ethnic groups and nations. So new "rituals" must be formed. Two examples can help to elucidate how difficult this task is.

We mentioned earlier that when German Chancellor Willy Brandt went to Poland on a state visit he also laid a wreath at the memorial of the Warsaw uprising. But instead of copying the accustomed ritual of bowing his head as a gesture of respect, he fell to his knees. Brandt changed the traditional "liturgy" of acknowledgment by choosing a gesture that was not among the ritualized gestures of collective communication between nations.

Not surprisingly, this unprecedented act became an immediate source of dispute. Many welcomed the kneeling down of a leading German politician as a valuable expression of official repentance. Marek Edelmann, a survivor of the Warsaw uprising, spoke for many: "That was a great thing... With this gesture the Germans honoured the victims at the moral level. The Germans who had murdered knelt down in front of their victims."[1] Edelmann's remark expressed the symbolic representativeness of Brandt's gesture: he saw "the Germans" collectively kneeling in front of their victims.

There is another aspect which merits attention here. Brandt was known to have been part of the resistance against the Nazis. He had spent the twelve years of the Third Reich in exile in Scandinavia, returning to his native country only after 1945. At the strictly personal level, then, he could have argued that he had no obligation to repent for the guilt of the Nazis. Yet he understood that as chancellor of the Federal Republic of Germany he had to face the entire history of his country. As one observer remarked, "the one who did not need to do it knelt down for all who need to but do not kneel, because they do not dare or because they cannot bring themselves to or because they cannot dare to do it."[2] This element of vicariousness in Brandt's gesture made it even more remarkable and convincing.

The Polish people and the majority of the German people appropriated this act as a symbolic expression of public contrition. It was understood as a disarming gesture and thus as an expression of historical correction. It paved the way for the famous *Ostpolitik*, which led to a normalization of relationships between Germany and its neighbours in Eastern Europe.

Nevertheless, a sizeable part of the German population considered Brandt's gesture as inappropriate. They felt that he had betrayed the dignity of the nation. They were the ones who also criticized Brandt's *Ostpolitik* as a "sell-out", arguing that he should never have given up German territorial claims to areas east of the Oder-Neisse line which had been taken over by Poland and the Soviet Union after the second world war. But Brandt was convinced that the historic guilt of the Nazi period needed to be corrected by voluntary and unmistakable acts of renunciation. He knew that the humiliation of the nations which had been occupied by German troops required some kind of restoration. The hurt of the peoples had to be faced. Their sufferings needed recognition if they were to lose their bitter sting.

Although Willy Brandt was a secularized Protestant and never professed to be an active Christian, he introduced elements of forgiveness into politics. Both his symbolic gesture in Warsaw and his practical *Ostpolitik* indicated his commitment to healing the wounds of the past in order to inaugurate a better future. He sensed that relationships of trust can rest only on the foundations of equality and justice, and that these require significant acts of renunciation and correction.

We will look further at the criterion of renunciation in the next chapter when we deal with the relationship between forgiving and giving up. Here we are concerned with the symbolic expression of aspects of forgiveness between collectives. This brings us to a second example from recent German history.

In 1985, Chancellor Helmut Kohl was instrumental in setting up a political ritual to celebrate the normality and reconciliation achieved between Germany and the USA. President Reagan agreed to join Kohl in a visit to a war cemetery in Bitburg. The idea was that the leaders of these two nations would join hands across the graves of soldiers of the second world war, to symbolize that this hurtful past had lost its hurtful and dividing character. But what was intended to be a symbolic celebration of reconciliation turned out to be a symbol of continued pain. What happened?

When suggesting Bitburg, Kohl had not taken into consideration the fact that among those buried there were members of the infamous SS. Not surprisingly, survivors of the Holocaust cried out in anger and bitterness against the idea that the US president and German chancellor would celebrate a normality that symbolically appeared to sanction Nazi atrocities. While these protests did not succeed in cancelling the "Bitburg handshake", it took place with less fanfare than originally intended and never achieved the persuasive power it was meant to have.

The mistake behind this ritual was that it claimed normality without asking the victims whether they felt ready for it. It was simply assumed that forty years was long enough for everyone to lay the past to rest. But as we have said, the mere flow of time does not heal anything. The memories of the victims follow a different rhythm from those of the perpetrators. While the latter are only too eager to forget, the former are bound to their sufferings in many ways.

It has also been argued that the Bitburg handshake ritual was to symbolize a new claim of normality regarding the deployment of German troops beyond the strict limitations set out by NATO and to prepare the ground for more active German involvement in the United Nations, including military participation in UN peace-keeping missions. On this interpretation, the acknowledgment of normality would have freed the German military establishment from the shadows of the second world war. This was in the interest not only of those Germans who wished to "let bygones be bygone" but also of other nations that wanted to involve Germany more directly in emerging geo-strategic schemes to secure the resources and power-bases of the global market.

In any case, it is revealing to compare Brandt's gesture of kneeling in Warsaw with the image of Reagan and Kohl shaking hands at Bitburg. Both intended to speak at the transnational level about some vital and painful aspects of a shared past. But their messages were decidedly different. Brandt's gesture was an act of recognition that asked nothing in return, a silent plea for reconciliation. The handshake in Bitburg was a gesture that claimed mutuality and was meant to show that reconciliation had been achieved. The former took seriously the feelings of the other side, whereas the latter took solidarity for granted and thereby provoked angry resentment.

Both gestures show how great is the need to cultivate symbolic communication between peoples in full appreciation of the difficulties involved. Even with the best of intentions misunderstandings are unavoidable, for collectives encompass a great variety of opinions. We need to work towards a more precise *grammar of deep remembering*; in other words, the public must be trained to learn a new code of symbolic conduct that reflects our transnational values and objectives. There is a growing discrepancy between our ethnocentric symbolic codes and the reality of our transnational interdependence. Our collective identities are at a level that does not adequately correspond with the realities of our daily lives, notably in the areas of economics, science, the arts and the media.

The art of remembering requires a new kind of literacy that aims at developing an adequate awareness of the historical legacies of other peoples and the depth of our mutual involvement. If it is in their memories that peoples form their sense of their own selves as well as their images of others, then it is only in sharing such memories that they will be able to reach new images of togetherness and mutual accountability.

Obviously, working for such images of connectedness must be regarded as a vital component of politics. It is part of public culture and of "public relations", in the best sense of that term. It should not be left to develop at random. What steps and processes are needed to improve this work?

Walking through history together

Joseph Montville argues convincingly that ethnic groups and peoples which have been at war with each other and thus harbour profound resentments against each other must engage in walking through their histories together. He suggests that representative groups be set up to revisit each other's history, especially those events that are still hurting. Careful and patient attention is required to listen to the interpretations of those events by the "enemy" side in order to begin to appreciate the depth of pain and the extent of resentment. To put this in terms of Volkan's image of the "canopy", the process Montville suggests is to invite the "enemies" to mutual visitations with the aim of slowly spreading out a new canopy wide enough to provide shelter for both sides, or at least to facilitate sufficient exchange between the two camps to avoid new misinterpretations.

There have been some efforts to facilitate such joint "walks through history". For example, a German-Polish schoolbook commission was set up to remove from textbooks in Germany and Poland those images and interpretations which fostered traditional stereotypes of the enemy. Similar processes have been suggested for Croats and Serbs, or for Estonians and Russians. Many more examples could be found to elucidate the urgency of such work. To enter into processes of rereading and rewriting our histories together is a conscious form of re-membering or, to put it more prudently, a careful way of overcoming the accustomed patterns of dis-membering one people from the other.

This task would appear most urgent among ethnic groups and peoples which live side by side, often claiming the same lands. Ireland is a typical case. But it is not only among enemy-neighbours that efforts of re-membering history together must go on. The history of slavery, for instance, is a vast area of concern going beyond national histories and connecting entire continents. It is not enough to declare that slavery was abolished long ago (though it continues in some forms to this day). The historical impact of slavery is still with us. European nations have great difficulty facing up to the fact that for centuries a considerable part of their economic success and scientific and cultural wealth derived from the slave trade. This binds them to the African peoples much more deeply than they wish to acknowledge and should compel them to create political options that would contribute to the gradual healing of Africa's miseries.

For Africa continues to suffer from the aftermath of slavery. We need only to mention the centuries of "brain-drain", the disruption of traditional societies and the corruption of those African rulers who allowed themselves to be bought into the trade. Beyond these obvious economic and social ills lie the deeper evils of unresolved humiliation, shame and anger which are bound to have a profound impact on how Africans deal with Europeans.

Here we cannot even begin to sketch the implications of this historical scourge. But reference must also be made to the impacts of slave-culture on economic relations, social patterns and cultural and religious traditions in Brazil, the Caribbean and the United States. What kind of re-membering is needed to face at least the disastrous legacies of slavery? How can the different sectors of society — the economy, the academy, the religious institutions — learn to respond to the ways they have been shaped by it?

Transnational discourse does not even have the vocabulary to speak to these issues. We have not even begun to work out symbolic expressions of corporate recognition and repentance; and gestures such as Willy Brandt's have remained the exception.

The kind of act required is hinted at in a remark by Bishop Lesslie Newbigin after a visit to Elmira Castle on the coast of Ghana, which was a stronghold of British colonial rule and a centre of the slave-trade. Newbigin was particularly appalled to discover that not only was the chapel of this castle built directly over the dungeon where the slaves were kept before being shipped off to America, but that a hole was cut in the chapel floor so that the British at prayer could keep an eye on the captured Africans. He writes: "I am always amazed that these crimes can be so easily forgotten. Ever since that visit I have wished that some representative Englishman — an archbishop or prime minister — might come to Ghana and go down into that dungeon, kneel down on the floor and offer a prayer of contrition. I still hope it may happen."[3]

Following what was said in the previous chapter, it cannot be generally expected of national leaders to lead their nations in such acts of public acknowledgment. Persons at the intermediate levels — well-known academics or religious leaders — are needed who will face up to such tasks first. Their vicarious recognition may pave the way towards processes of deep remembering which will eventually include national leaders and spread towards the general public. We need intermediary groups to start these various walks through history together. We need opportunities for committed persons, including youth, to interpret to each other how it feels to have to live with a certain history.

The task of deep remembering calls for new schools, for ways of learning from each other across ethnic, racial and cultural divides. It calls for forms of sharing that deliberately transcend accustomed patterns of academic exchange and seek to build bridges between the hearts. The art of remembering calls for a new educational awareness, interpretative skills and methods. We are not suggesting that people should give up their national and ethnic canopies. But people need to create some space between their canopies so that they can meet each other without "trespassing".

Connecting signs and symbols

When the French-German friendship treaty was concluded, a wide range of practical cooperation was agreed upon. The governments decided to establish patterns of regular consultation; an exchange programme for youth was inaugurated; many partnerships between French and German towns and cities were set up. Yet it was not decided to establish a joint day of remembering. As a lasting symbolic expression of this unprecedented historical achievement, such a day could have created public space for a variety of groups to celebrate aspects of this friendship and to deal with critical developments and misunderstandings. Thus an opportunity was missed to create *connecting symbols* which might have helped to plant this new friendship into the memories of both nations. After more than 25 years, the practical cooperation between the two countries seems to be functioning satisfactorily at the political and bureaucratic levels, but certain emotional uncertainties and doubts linger on.

I am not suggesting that the respective national holidays should be replaced by joint holidays. But there are ways of adding new meaning to existing national festivals and consciously reducing any chauvinistic tendencies that may creep into the celebrations. Remembering is an active process; the content of the events which a nation chooses to remember can and must be appropriated anew in each new situation. For example, it is possible to introduce into existing national feast days new aspects that underscore the relationships with neighbouring countries and to reduce elements of the traditional celebrations that are offensive to them. Tendencies to make jokes based on racial or national differences should also be discouraged. Patriotism may have its noble features, but it is certainly risky, especially when evoked by political leaders to solicit or justify sacrifices from "ordinary" men and women. National pride may be understandable but it must never be nurtured and exploited at the cost of other nations.

Precisely because the art of remembering is directly related to political issues, it cannot be left to politicians alone. I have referred above to the significant educational dimensions involved here. This means that the development and nurture of remembering depends largely on the awareness of the public sector or what is often called the civil society, giving special importance to social groups and associations which recognize the connectedness of human beings and work for those concerns which they have in common, irrespective of national boundaries, religious differences, gender and race.

In addition to the critical reappropriation of existing national holidays and rituals, deep remembering requires the creation of new connecting symbols. The United Nations has done a great deal in this respect by establishing specific "days" for global concerns (though it has perhaps established too many, for an inflation of remembrance days weakens the idea itself). Among these, Human Rights Day (10 December) is of special significance. It should be celebrated as an important transnational holiday, because one cannot overvalue the great effort to formulate universal standards of the rights to which each human being is entitled. The fact that these rights are being violated all the time only adds to their importance and underlines the need to anchor them soundly in the memories of all nations.

Like Human Rights Day, United Nations Day (24 October) should also be celebrated. While much of the criticism of the UN and its various institutions is justified, there is simply no alternative to it. Therefore, it needs all the support it can get. And if, as many critics have charged, the United Nations has fallen into the hands of bureaucrats, a major reason for that is perhaps that we, the citizens across the globe, have lost our enthusiasm and withdrawn our emotional support and dedication for it. Certainly it is exhausting to "think globally", as the slogan goes, because the complexities and apparent ungovernability of the global situation wear us down. But it is precisely because of the tension between the indispensability of the UN and the feeling that its mission seems impossible that we require certain recurrent days to rethink our problems and recommit ourselves to the daunting tasks.

As much as we need Human Rights Day and United Nations Day to affirm the advances and achievements of the human community, we need a *global day of remembrance* to remember and grieve the catastrophes and sufferings of the world. Some have suggested 6 August, which reminds the world of the bombing of Hiroshima, which marked the beginning of the permanent threat to human history from the possibilities of nuclear destruction. Others would suggest 30 April, which is designated in Israel as Holocaust Day. For one minute on that day, all activity in the country comes to a complete halt. This moment creates the necessary space to remember again the Holocaust victims. Might such a day not be turned into a worldwide day of remembrance of human beings all over the earth who have been and continue to be tortured, burned, massacred, so that out of such grieving could arise the spirit of resistance against every form of concentration camp, ethnic cleansing, genocide and massacre? Auschwitz stands for crimes of singular proportions; yet the Jewish people do not "own" Auschwitz. As the Jewish poet Primo Levi put it, Auschwitz has turned into a "contagious illness". Its cancerous proliferations have reappeared in South Africa, in Uganda and Rwanda, in Guatemala and Cambodia.

Not only would a global Remembrance and Resistance Day help people to see across their traditional boundaries what human beings are capable of doing to each other, but it would also enable them to realize that human beings have it within themselves to rise above the murderous excesses of violence and to liberate each other from the chains of retaliation. The wounds of all the peoples must be remembered, for each death is unique. All nations need healing.

We have suggested that national holidays can to some extent be "rebaptized" in order to assume new and additional meanings. A similar process must also happen with places that have engraved themselves into the human memory as places of extreme horror. For me as a German one such place is Auschwitz. More than a geographical location at which human beings were extinguished mercilessly, it is the symbol of an entire system of domination and extinction. For other members of the human race other places stand out with equal sharpness: Wounded Knee and Sharpeville, Bhopal and Guernica, Grosny and Goma. We have already mentioned Hiroshima; we might also mention Chernobyl. Both have changed from being specific locations on the world map to places on the symbolic map of humanity's nuclear folly.

The salient point is that all such places remind us of the transnational character of human violence. Auschwitz concerns not only Jews and Germans, Hiroshima cannot be reduced to the war between the United States and Japan, Chernobyl is not just the heritage of the Russians and the Ukrainians. There is a connectedness of evil that touches every human being and reaches forward to have an impact on future generations. Therefore it is of paramount importance for the human race to accept these and similar places as symbols of shared pain and shared responsibility. Only as we learn to face the violence can we hope to overcome it.

All these suggestions confront us with a profound dilemma summed up in the question of whether the human heart is capable of feeling so much pain. Our ethical energies do not seem to match our violence. With our scientific, technological and economic capacities we have set up tremendous projects to which our ethical imagination appears not to have enough time and strength to respond. In recent years, these intellectual and administrative skills have turned this vast globe into one single world. So "globalization" — which creates an increasing number of victims for increasingly fewer winners — is a fact of life at the end of this millennium. But the same human beings who have made this system possible seem unable to live up to its emotional impact and ethical challenges. Their heart is not where their intelligence has taken them.

One aspect of this dilemma is that "globalization" is a project of an intellectual and economic élite which the majority of humanity must accept as inevitable and beyond its control, a development to be suffered. The widespread emotional and ethical numbing of our times may be seen as a symptom of victimization and helplessness. These widespread and amorphous experiences of victimization may lead people into withdrawal movements of various kinds. Privatism, exaggerated individualism, fundamentalism, consumerism — all such "isms" can and should be understood as expressions of emotional exhaustion.

I have argued throughout this book that deep remembering is about taking the victims seriously. This is the only way to rescue the profound importance of forgiveness from its many cheap distortions. Thus one way of responding creatively to the dilemma of "globalization" is to try to understand the processes of victimization which it produces and to relate these new experiences to the patterns in which we have been trained to organize our identities. This is a task that requires space.

This is one of the reasons why we need to work for the space of transnational symbols, signs and feast days. We must get beyond the ethnocentric and nationalistic forms of remembering which are based on and reinforce simplified perceptions of the past. In underlining the complexities of shared remembering we want to strengthen the awareness of peoples of their connectedness and similarities, which far exceed their differences. It is possible and timely to celebrate together, to learn a few songs together, to respect and venerate the same great teachers of the human race, to broaden thereby the awareness of our common human canopy.

The growing disenchantment of many women and men with centres of political and economic power like Washington or Brussels or New York can also be understood as an indication of the increasing discrepancy between technological and economic superstructures on the one hand and the emotional capacities of comprehension on the other. There is a discrepancy between the electronic, economic and financial networks which encircle the globe and the continued nursing of national, religious and even racial ideologies and idiosyncrasies at the local and regional levels. While it is unrealistic to assume that all inhabitants of this globe can and will develop a global consciousness, the general line should and must be to underscore the connectedness of all human beings.

There is certainly much reason to celebrate the variety of cultures and customs and the richness and splendour they contribute to our world. But such variety should never be interpreted in such a way as to justify polarization and strife. As the indispensable "playgrounds" of human imagination, all cultures need and deserve their own space. But they should not be regarded as being mutually exclusive or incompatible. It was the fatal error of the cold war to divide the world into Eastern and Western blocs; it obscured awareness of each other and impaired the underlying connectedness for forty years. Equally dangerous would be the much-discussed "clash of civilizations" which the Harvard historian Samuel Huntington sees as the prospect for the coming century. The great varieties of expression and form, the internal disparities as well as the overlap of these civilizations defy such simplifications. One need only refer here to the connectedness which the sciences and the arts, and music in particular, have helped to create among all the peoples of the world.

The guiding model for politics should not be the "clash" but connectedness, not insistence on separate identities but training in inclusiveness. We have many differences, but we have much more in common. We are many, but we are also one.

NOTES

[1] Quoted by Guido Knapp, *Die grossen Fotos des Jahrhunderts: Bilder die Geschichte machen*, Munich, 1994, p.164.
[2] *Ibid.*
[3] Quoted by Brian Frost, *The Politics of Peace*, p.149.

11. Forgiving and Giving Up
in Political Life

In the previous chapter we spoke of Willy Brandt's kneeling in front of the Warsaw memorial as a symbolic expression of public, representative and vicarious repentance and a reflection of his *Ostpolitik*, the determination to build more trusting relations between Germany and its neighbours in Eastern Europe. We also mentioned that Brandt was attacked in some quarters for giving up Germany's territorial claims east of the Oder-Neisse demarcation line. To renounce an option and voluntarily give up a piece of bargaining power was regarded as a foolish thing for a politician to do. Brandt was convinced, however, that Germany's claims to its former territories had to be given up, not simply as a matter of political expediency (there was no way of getting them back without engaging in yet another suicidal war), but as a matter of historical justice. He knew that without some kind of correction there would be no way forward.

Hence, if Brandt's kneeling in Warsaw was the equivalent of what would be called in classical theological terms *confessio oris*, "confession with the mouth", his *Ostpolitik* can similarly be compared to an act of *satisfactio operis*, "satisfaction by works". But it would not be adequate to describe this programme simply in terms of restitution. Brandt was certainly interested in setting things right again, but he pursued this task by giving up past claims for the sake of clearing the space for new covenants.

Creating new spaces:
the relationship between forgiving and giving up

As we reflect on the possibility for forgiveness to become an integral part of politics, it is important to understand that this has to do with creating new space between partners who are too close to each other. The term "space" is not used here in a geographical sense, which would imply policies of "ethnic cleansing" and apartheid, but metaphorically to refer to new spaces in the consciousness of people. It is the political imagination that requires new space in order to come up with fresh solutions.

It is helpful in this context to refer again to Anwar Sadat. By travelling to Jerusalem he created new space within which his own people and the people of Israel were able to discover alternatives to war and retaliation. He did so by consciously giving up the traditional claims of Arab people to all the land occupied by Israel. He abandoned the ideology of enmity, which had held Arab people hostage to the fateful and futile politics of war. Convinced that there must be space in the Middle East for Israelis and Arabs to live side by side, he embarked on the struggle for reconciliation and transcended the accustomed political categories that prevented Arabs from recognizing Israel as a fact on the landscape of the Middle East. By leaving the trenches of denial he created space for recognition of the obvious, namely that Israel was there to stay and that the needs and aspirations of all partners in that region had to be taken seriously. What was even more important is that Sadat's leaving his trenches enabled Israelis to leave theirs and to begin to see the Arab peoples not as eternal enemies but as factual neighbours and potential friends.

The subtle mutuality between forgiving and giving up is also evident in a letter I received in November 1993 from Ratu Meli Vesikula, an indigenous chief in Fiji, who wrote to me about his own experience of restitution and forgiveness:

> In the racial violence in my country following the two military coups of 1987, I stood up strongly for the cause of my people using violent means to gain the upper hand against Indian people who made up the second major race in Fiji.
>
> In 1988, I found a change of heart through the help of a church minister first of all, and later through coming in contact with men and women from Moral Rearmament. Through change, I found new humility and obedience, which eventually led me to apologize publicly to Indian leaders and leaders of other races in Fiji for my part in the violence, and to my own people for leading them in the wrong direction. Their forgiveness of me gave birth to a new spirit, literally, which was so powerful in bringing about healing and reconciliation among different

peoples of Fiji. As the spirit grew, trust was rebuilt and barriers taken down, leaders began to talk and govern fairly, and stability and security returned.

This incident was a big factor in Fiji going beyond violence to a caring and sharing society, and the restoration of democracy through our first general election last year...

There is much more to be done... to ensure that this spirit of forgiveness lives and thrives in the hearts of our people for always. Of course we have problems, but the spirit of restitution and forgiveness is helping to rebuild and reinforce the moral fibre of our nation, which will ensure a brighter future for our children...

The public apology marked the turning point. With his confession Chief Vesikula gave up the violent racial struggle. He accepted responsibility for having led his own people in the wrong direction and thereby bringing harm to them and to other racial groups in Fiji. By abandoning the option of violent power the chief disarmed himself. He thus made room for new political solutions to appear. In his words, his confession "gave birth to a new spirit". His humility provided the space for generosity and magnanimity to emerge on all sides of the conflict, which helped to restore stable and secure conditions in his country.

In religious terms, the profound change of perspective that enabled Chief Vesikula to make this disarming move was a conversion experience. In his own words: "It dawned on me that God loves everybody, that we are all absolutely equal... Slowly I realized that everyone in Fiji was important to its development." Here is a typical example of a person moving beyond the canopy of ethnic identity to discover the wider human canopy that encompasses everyone.

Creating space in our consciousness for forgiveness requires leaving behind accustomed patterns of enmity which captivate our imagination and lead us again and again to seek revenge and retaliation. Brandt, Sadat and Chief Vesikula succeeded in moving beyond the sterile patterns that divide the world into friends and foes, good and bad, "us" and "them". To give up such options is not to surrender bargaining power, but to create it. By their astonishing moves these three quite different political leaders helped to "decontaminate" poisoned and hurtful relationships between ethnic groups and nations. They began to recognize the "enemies" as the victims of their enmity and to see them in their own right as equal and necessary partners for the construction of reliable relationships. By removing some of the roots of their own people's hatreds and suspicions, they cleared a place for trusting deliberation and constructive cooperation. They knew that unless the injustices and the wounds of the past were addressed in decisive ways they would continue to haunt any prospect of a peaceful solution.

Dealing with stolen power

The failure to recognize the category of renunciation as a constitutive element in politics betrays a limited understanding of power and power-politics. Our political life suffers from the false beliefs that power, no matter how it was gained, must be defended at all costs and that one must always negotiate from a position of strength and never appear to be opening a "window of vulnerability".

If politics — the "art of the possible" — depends, as we have said, on the "art of remembering", the way we look at power must be guided by the question of how and from whom it was acquired. The relationship between power and victimization needs more serious consideration than it has been given.

The power of every nation has its genesis and history and can never be separated from its impact on other groups and peoples. Like all other kinds of power, that of national or ethnic collectives is "trespassing" by its very nature, that is, it is constantly stepping over the boundaries that are set. No living entity generates its power simply and exclusively in and by itself; all depend on others, absorb some of their energies, but also share part of their energies with others. These constant processes of giving and taking, sharing and stealing explain why power, including political power, is such an intensely ambivalent challenge in any ethical discourse.

Essentially, politics is about seeking to establish systems by which the interests of the various agents of power can be controlled and balanced. This implies reducing as much as possible the tendencies to victimize certain groups, so as not to upset the power-play between the different subjects. To affirm that societies must work for justice is in fact to say that they must strive to keep the number of victims as small as possible. The great and lasting achievement of democratic systems is the attempt to establish a balance of powers by which the processes of trespassing and victimization remain under control. Such democratic systems have drawn the lessons of bitter social conflicts and revolutions against autocratic, absolutist or oligarchic forms of government: that victimized groups will not stay quiet forever but will tend to resort to violence if the power that is by nature theirs is denied to them.

Democratic societies have thus incorporated the insight that it is essential for some parties to renounce part of their power so that there is sufficient space for all to develop their potential. How a society looks after its weakest members is the best indicator of its capacity to balance the powers of all its subjects.

What is true within nations is also true between them. The founders of the European Community saw clearly that a larger unity could be established only if all partners were willing to give up some of their sovereignty. The goals of lasting peace in Europe required a good deal of renunciation. But in recent years this compelling insight of a generation of political leaders who vividly remembered the excesses of two world wars has lost much of its weight. Much of the recent critique of European union is rooted in anxiety over the possible loss of national power, and most of its justification is based on the will to establish a new power bloc on the global level. There is little room here for seeing the productive aspects of renunciation. Instead, this aggressive self-centredness, coupled with nervousness about the global power-play, prevents many Europeans from adequately remembering the abuse of power in their own history.

A case in point is the continued denial of the guilt-ridden chapters of European expansionism in other parts of the world, accompanied by the facile assumption that colonialism ended on the date the former colonies gained political independence. We have already noted that much of Europe's "progress" and wealth are related to the abominations of the slave trade. And to this day European powers reap political, economic and cultural benefits from their former colonies in many obvious and subtle ways. The suppressed guilt-feelings of Europeans and the lasting impacts of victimization in the hearts and minds of the formerly colonialized and enslaved peoples continue to exert a debilitating influence on the consciousness and imagination of their leaders and account for many irritations, fears, insecurities and suspicions.

The history of Europe and the United States with Central and South America is another case in point. It is not enough to refer to the theft of the gold of the Incas or the depletion of the silver mines in Potosí. The angry and hurtful experiences of impoverishment and disempowering extend deep into the realms of the unconscious and call for profound corrections. When the 500th anniversary of the voyage of Columbus was commemorated in 1992, the issue of restitution was raised by some embittered and angry Latin Americans. They calculated that the gains realized by the European nations from 500 years of exploitation amounted to a staggering sum, on which they based their demands for compensation. Similar claims for restitution of stolen lands and resources have been made by Native Americans in the US.

All of this has been to no avail. Nowhere does the political establishment accept the notion of compensation for historical injustices. Nor does the legal basis for such measures exist, and it would be difficult to establish even if the will to do so were present. Only in the case of declared wars can the winners force the losers to make retributions. Compensation is thus associated with defeat, not with sovereignty. It is a symbol of weakness, not strength.

But wars are not the only instrument by which nations steal power. There are many ways for people to aggrandize themselves at the expense of others; indeed, it seems that the mighty nations of today no longer need to go to war in order to get hold of other nations' resources. Full-scale wars with their massive annihilative power are counter-productive. The kind of warfare that goes on at the end of this century is in the marketplace. Above all, it is the undeclared war of external debt, which is taking a devastatingly high toll in human lives and ecological destruction. What is benignly called "globalization" is in fact a worldwide war against eighty percent of the population of the planet and the earth itself. The processes of victimization it has set in motion are of such proportions that the inevitable violent reactions will resemble the horrors of the apocalypse.

Before we turn our attention to this, it is necessary to address the question of whether "restitution" is an adequate category. Is it at all possible? Even if nations were willing to make amends for past injustices, could they ever expect to *make good* what has been destroyed?

The wheel of history cannot be turned back. The impact of past injustices cannot be undone. Such heinous acts as the destruction of African societies or the annihilation of the Inca empire cannot be repaired. We have already discussed this bitter truth with regard to the Holocaust. But although terms like "restitution" and "compensation" suggest that it is possible to correct the past, the result, whenever this has been attempted, has invariably been frustrating. Since nothing can ever be enough to heal the wounds of the past, material and financial compensation often even deepens the bitterness of the survivors.

Yet there is a profound need to take the category of compensation seriously. Not only is it the tangible expression of the perpetrators' recognition of past injustices and their commitment to move beyond them; even more importantly, it implies that the victims are recognized as subjects in their own right. Their value as equal partners in the process of facing the damages of past evils is acknowledged and established.

The notion of compensation implies that the victims have been recognized as partners in a new search. But what is this search about? In my judgment compensations make sense when they are designed not to repair the past but to prepare for the future, to de-victimize the victims and create conditions in which they can again become independent subjects of their future.

In the previous chapter I remarked that symbolic expressions of guilt are a precondition for creating a new sense of connectedness. Denial of historical guilt always deepens the impact of victimization and increases the likelihood of violent reaction. But when past evil is addressed, it loses its poisonous presence and makes room for practical measures which can initiate productive steps forward and inaugurate fresh solutions.

Acts of deep remembering lead to covenants. The disarming gestures by the three political leaders mentioned earlier clearly opened the space for people who had been in conflict with each other to regard each other as partners.

A substantial part of the compensations paid by the Federal Republic of Germany to the survivors of the Holocaust went not to individual Jews but to the state of Israel. The state of Israel was of vital relevance for determining the future of the Jewish people. So the compensations were not strictly aimed at repairing the damage done to the immediate victims of the Nazi era, but at inaugurating political developments that would create a greater sense of security for the Jewish people in general.

The partners to the covenants of which we are speaking here are certainly equal in trust and dignity, but not in a material sense. So the covenants are made to work for this kind of equalization. They are schemes of burden-sharing, in which unjust and stolen power is given up in order to correct inequalities.

This is not a politics of altruism, but rather a politics based on a deepened awareness of the inextricable connectedness of everything that is done, good and evil alike, a politics based on the wisdom that comes from seeing oneself with the eyes of the other. Such wisdom is in the interests of all; for it knows that victimization is bound to become a threat to the well-being of all unless something is done to redeem it.

As nations begin to see the impact of their power-plays from the viewpoint of the victims, they can learn to use their strength for sharing burdens and relieving pain. Forgiveness in politics is about creating space for a safer future.

Forgiveness in the global village

It is often said that the world has become a "global village". The examples given to substantiate this generally refer to the instant availability of news from all corners of the globe and the easy accessibility of all major cities for the international traveller. In fact, this metaphor is highly misleading, for it reflects the perspective of a very small élite, while the overwhelming majority of the world's population still see the earth as a vast expanse far beyond their comprehension, much less their control. The presence of Coca-Cola in the remotest places is not an indication of cosmopolitan consciousness but a symbol of the amorphous powers that impress themselves on people everywhere, adding to their sense of helplessness and disloca-tion.

Coca-Cola and McDonalds and CNN symbolize a process which the overwhelming majority of the world can experience only as massive victimization. A staggering news report in 1996 disclosed that 358 women and men own as much as fifty percent of the entire global population. Globalization accelerates existing processes of marginalization and connects and centralizes them at the global level.

The most explosive and devastating expression of this phenomenon today is the debt crisis. While we cannot discuss it in detail here, we may note that it is basically the result of four interacting processes.

1. During the 1960s, the emerging global consciousness was expressed in terms of "development". Countries were seen as either "developed" or "underdeveloped"; and it was assumed that financial, technical and material transfers from the haves to the have-nots could overcome the existing disparity and poverty. Rereading the declarations of those years, one is struck by their idealistic and hopeful tone. Overcoming poverty was considered to be a matter of only a few years.

In those years wealthy nations and international banking consortiums made loans to "underdeveloped" countries with the aim of building up profitable industries which would enable these countries to enter the world market and quickly repay their debts. Little attention was given to the social, cultural, religious and educational prerequisites for such speedy industrialization. There was an exaggerated expectation that the products of these industries would fetch high prices on international markets. Nor was there sufficient recognition of the fact that the industrialized nations would not stop and wait for the others to catch up but would continue to move ahead into other areas, so that the existing disparities would continue.

2. The consequences of these unheeded realities emerged when the time came to service these debts. The processes of industrialization took longer than anticipated, their products could not compete and consequently the income was disappointing. A good deal of money was siphoned off by corrupt élites in the poor countries whose ordinary citizens had to pay the bill. To make things worse, the oil crisis in the early 1970s drastically upset global financial arrangements. The prices for resources like oil rocketed to unimaginable heights, while the prices for raw materials like coffee, tea and bananas plummeted. Under these conditions, the interest on the loans could be only partially repaid. The loans had to be renegotiated, and thus began the perilous spiral of indebtedness.

3. The growing economic imbalances increased the disparities between strong and weak currencies, leading to drastic changes in

interest rates, which brought the already existing debts to staggering heights. The international monetary institutions, backed by the most powerful nations, the Group of Seven industrialized states (G-7), began to impose policies of "readjustment" on the indebted countries, forcing them to sell whatever could be sold (thus increasing pressures on the labour force and on environmental resources) and to reduce state expenses (weakening and dismantling the meagre educational, social and health services that did exist).

4. In the 1990s this neo-liberal monetarism has turned into what some have called "turbo-capitalism". With the help of global deregulation measures, ever-increasing sums of money float freely around the globe, ruthlessly exploiting even the smallest variations in national interest rates or gambling on anticipated changes. This global financial market puts all national economies under the merciless pressure of having to compete with each other over their share in the production of goods and services. Some nations, such as the so-called Asian Tigers, are temporarily profiting from this competition, though at an alarming cost to their poor and to their environment. Overall, this battle has led to a large increase in unemployment all over the world and has plunged poorer countries into chaos and disintegration.

It goes without saying that there are more aspects to this than can be presented in a brief overview, and that each country faces a particular specific combination of these factors. But as external debts have reached astronomical proportions, more money is flowing from impoverished countries to the donor institutions than they are receiving, yet there is no hope of ever leaving the debt trap. It is clear that these economic policies contribute heavily to the destruction of the very future of entire regions of the world. The future of coming generations is being stolen from them.

The debt crisis is an alarming example of how processes of trespassing and victimization have reached global proportions. What is needed are policies on how these debts can be forgiven. The debtor countries urgently require space to rebuild their economic and social infrastructures; instead, they have "readjustment plans" imposed on them by international financial institutions, which serve to protect the interests of the creditors and thus prolong the debt wars and the processes of victimization.

There can be no just peace in a world in which twenty percent do well while eighty percent are left to die. But this peace requires serious attempts by the receiving nations to give up their stolen power and to create space in which new social and economic solutions can appear. Again, this is not a matter of altruistic generosity, but a matter of political realism and enlightened self-interest; for if globalization continues in this turbo-capitalistic way it will inevitably lead to violent social and ecological reactions such as the human race has never seen.

Although I earlier criticized the metaphor of the "global village", there is one sense in which it is appropriate. The people of a village know where their village ends. They know their boundaries. And they know that they are in it together. We who are living today are the first generations of humans who have been able to look at the earth from outside and see it for what it is: a small planet wrapped in thin layers of air, a precious blue ark of amazing life lost in the dark expanses of the universe. Looking at our planet as our one and single home is new and frightening to many, although the myths of ancient cultures have always known this.

As more and more people begin to be sensitive to the amazing connectedness of all of life on this precious finite planet earth, they come to see the folly and stupidity of the dominant political and economic paradigm by which humans destroy the basis on which depends their own survival, as well as that of many other life forms. As the third millennium nears, we begin to see that the model of domination must be replaced by the paradigm of inhabitation. We are rediscovering what it means not to lord over the earth but to inhabit it in intense conviviality with the myriad other communities of life which were here long before we arrived on the scene and which have made it such a splendid home for us who have come along very late.

As the global village gets crowded there is simply no longer enough space for the politics of domination. The world has not been created to make money. Instead, we have to open our hands in an effort to reach out to each other and to solve our problems together.

For many it is already too late. Others, numbed by the amount of suffering and violence around them, have succumbed to despair. So it is time for women and men of good will within and beyond faith communities to come to each other's rescue and to re-member what is being torn apart.

We have tried to show that in its most profound sense forgiveness is about liberating people from the debilitating impasse of hurt and the desire to hurt in return. It is thus a process of re-membering which moves us from separation to community, from suspicion and confrontation to trust and mutuality. It is about creating space for perpetrators and victims to discover their common humanity and to covenant together for the sake of a safer, less violent future. In this sense forgiveness is about training to inhabit this world together.

So it is with a new sense of awe and surprise that we read the Beatitude: "Blessed are the meek, for they shall inherit the earth." The Aramaic word *l'makikhe* connotes gentleness, humility and softness — virtues considered utterly useless by the "tough guy" of today's world. Yet it is precisely the tough-guy mentality which wreaks havoc on the earth. There is a subtle truth in this Beatitude that we are beginning to see as we stand at the crossroads of the human adventure: either dominate the earth and thereby destroy it, or inhabit it with gentle, meek and humble hearts and be gifted with its riches. The choice is before us.

12. Truth and Reconciliation in South Africa

One of the truly amazing stories of contemporary history is surely the transition of Nelson Mandela from 27 years of imprisonment to the presidency of the Republic of South Africa. This change was brought about not by a violent revolutionary overthrow of the old régime but by negotiation and compromise. After more than 40 years, the National Party under F.W. de Klerk had finally come to realize that it could not sustain its apartheid policies. The African National Congress (ANC) under Mandela arrived at the decision that it would be in the nation's best interests to discontinue the armed struggle and instead to work out a negotiated settlement.

The National Unity and Reconciliation Act

One of the problems which had to be settled was how to deal with the legacy of the apartheid period. The ANC wanted a "Truth Commission", the National Party favoured a "Reconciliation Commission". The former were concerned about the victims of apartheid; the latter were looking for an amnesty for the perpetrators. The result was the National Unity and Reconciliation Act of 26 July 1995, which established the Truth and Reconciliation Commission (TRC).[1] It attempts to provide a concerted approach to apparently opposite interests. These are stated clearly in the Act's description of the "objectives of the Commission":

> The objectives of the Commission shall be to promote national unity and reconciliation in a spirit of understanding which transcends the conflicts and divisions of the past by
> a. establishing as complete a picture of the causes, nature and extent of the gross violations of human rights which were committed during the period from March 1, 1960, to the cut-off date, including the antecedents,

circumstances, factors and context of such violations, as well as the perspectives of the victims and the motives and perspectives of the persons responsible for the commission of the violations, by conducting investigations and holding hearings;

    b. facilitating the granting of amnesty to persons who make full disclosure of all the relevant facts relating to acts associated with a political objective and comply with the requirements of this Act;

    c. establishing and making known the fate or whereabouts of victims and restoring the human and civil dignity of such victims by granting them an opportunity to relate their own accounts of the violations of which they are the victims, and by recommending reparation measures in respect of them;

    d. compiling a report providing as comprehensive an account as possible of the activities and findings of the Commission... which contains recommendations of measures to prevent the future violations of human rights. [2]

The most important provisions of the Act can be summarized as follows:

1. It has been agreed to concentrate on the period from 1 March 1960, which would include the Sharpeville massacre, to the inauguration of President Mandela (see note 2). As to the nature of crimes to be investigated, the Act speaks of "gross human rights violations", by which are understood murder, attempted murder, abduction and torture.

2. A clear accent is placed on the restoration of the personal and civil dignity of the victims. This is underscored in section 11, which states that they must be treated with "compassion and respect". They must be permitted to present their own accounts of what happened to them or their relatives and they must receive help speedily.

This "victim-orientation" is clearly evident in the hearings. When the witnesses are led into the hearing room, all present stand up. The members of the TRC pose their questions in a careful and respectful manner. There are no cross-examinations. Interpreters are available so that the victims can speak and hear the questions in their own language. Usually a specially trained person is available to assist the witnesses as they relate their painful memories; for it is unavoidable that there should be tearful breakdowns. If witnesses feel that their safety is threatened, they can stay in specially rented apartments.

A vital element of this "victim-orientation" is the provision of material assistance to persons and families suffering badly because they have lost their breadwinners. The first six months of hearings made it clear that an interim aid programme is necessary; for there are many victims in such dire need of help that they cannot wait for the final decisions concerning pensions and other compensations, which will only be put in place after publication of the final report.

3. On the other hand, there is a clear intent to provide amnesty for all those persons who are prepared to give a detailed account of their activities, their background and motives. They need to prove beyond doubt that their acts were politically motivated. That cannot be done without naming those superiors responsible for giving the relevant orders. This has led to a gradual uncovering of the direct involvement of leading officers, prestigious party members, especially of the Inkatha Freedom Party, and National Party politicians, including former President P.W. Botha, who was named by General van der Merwe, former head of the South African Police, for having personally ordered the bombing of Khotso House, the headquarters of the South African Council of Churches.

4. The Act aims at a manner of investigation which avoids any kind of witch-hunt but contributes to transcending past divisions in a spirit of national unity in order to prevent the emergence of similar human rights violations in the future. There is a clear conviction that by looking at past injustices a safer way forward can be found.

Obviously, the Act brings together objectives which appear to be irreconcilable. How can the dignity of the victims ever be compatible with an amnesty for the perpetrators? How can one ensure that processes of painful remembering do not lead to renewed hatred but deepen mutual understanding?

It is clear that South Africa is engaged in an unprecedented exercise of "deep remembering". [3]

The struggle to heal the nation's memories

The prospect of as many as fifty or even a hundred thousand cases suggests the magnitude of the TRC's task. As the TRC spreads the net of hearings over each South African city and town, the contours of destruction created by apartheid emerge with growing clarity.

The daily horror

Each hearing produces new variations of the daily horror. Whether it is the cynicism of the "special branches" of the police force and their struggle against "communist terrorism", or the employment of 16,000 black "special constables" to instigate "black on black violence", or the dreadful disappearances and heinous tortures, or the bomb attacks and the "necklacing" — as these horrors are unearthed waves of shock flood through the land. Hardly a day goes by without some reference to the TRC in the media.

In October 1996, South African Television presented the documentary "Prime Evil", reconstructing the activities of a special murder squad whose operational base was a solitary farm called Vlakplaas. From there Eugene de Kock and his men committed assassinations and massacres all over Southern Africa, with the knowledge and support of leaders in top positions. "Prime Evil" produced deep anger, stunned confusion and shame. Now that Eugene de Kock has applied for amnesty, people are asking themselves in horror: Can such atrocities ever fall under an amnesty?

As other persons in top leadership positions appear before the Amnesty Committee, the pervasive and systemic violence of the apartheid era is disclosed in ever greater and more disturbing details. It is no longer possible to cling to the illusion that there was ever anything good in the idea of "separate development". White South Africans are beginning to realize that the persons they supported and wanted to believe in were in fact betraying them.

Apartheid's pervasive evil pollutes not only those directly implicated and maimed, not only the relatives of those police and politicians whose crimes are now being brought into the open. In some measure every South African feels hurt and defiled. Some react with bitter anger, others with bitter shame. How is it possible to talk about national unity and reconciliation when so much evil is in the air?

Catharsis

Some observers have described the work of the TRC as a cathartic process. They argue that this self-cleansing must inevitably lead to a turmoil of emotions. Anger, sadness, grief and shock must be allowed to surface. To face these profound emotions is the beginning of healing.

That assessment appears to be correct. Observing the hearings, one comes across something profoundly uplifting. As women and men recall their memories, they are again faced with all the pain and anguish. And yet, as they face up to their suffering and name it in public, they leave the witness stand with their heads held high. They have been recognized in their pain, and this is the beginning of a renewed dignity.

There is deep satisfaction, of course. Those destined to be annihilated are now praised as heroes. When they were tortured in the prisons, they were told: "Yell as loud as you wish; nobody will ever hear you!" Well, now the nation hears, and the accounts of their suffering are received into its memories. The voice of those who were made voiceless can now be heard on radio and television. The names of the torturers — who were beyond reproach only a few years ago — can now be mentioned openly. This correction of history is restoring for all who had been humiliated. The Magnificat of Mary comes to mind: "He has put down the mighty from their thrones, and exalted those of low degree" (Luke 1:52).

This profound satisfaction is not a subliminal form of revenge, but expresses itself in genuine readiness to forgive. Many victims repeat the phrase expressed by a witness during the first days of the hearings: "I am ready to forgive, but I need to know whom and for what."

Where are the whites?

This points to one of the central questions in the entire TRC process: "Cain, where are you? White brother, where are you? Don't you need to listen to Abel's story? Why do we not see you attending the hearings? Are you trying to pretend that you were not there when all this happened?"

Part of the reason white people are largely absent may be a deep sense of shame which causes them to avoid direct confrontation with the horrible facts. They may be afraid to be pilloried; they may even fear spontaneous acts of "necklacing" — which reflects the extent to which they have internalized their own propaganda which depicted blacks as incalculably brutal.

Naturally, in the prisons of shame excuses multiply. Barricades of "innocence" and indifference are erected: We did not do it! We did not know it! At least we did not want it to be done this way!

As we have noted earlier, it does happen that persons become desensitized when confronted with too much horror. Robert J. Lifton has written extensively about such "numbing".[4] Truth does not automatically liberate; it can also overwhelm and numb people. To face up to the truth of extreme guilt, human beings need to be held and comforted. The problem in a society like South Africa, so thoroughly steeped in racist patterns, is that white people seem unable to admit even the possibility that they might be held and comforted by black people.

Black analysts have suggested that white people have incorporated the "boss-client relationship" to such a degree that it does not even cross their mind to expect help from or to owe something to their inferiors. When blacks express their willingness to forgive, whites consider it something "normal" which corresponds with their client status. But the *baas* has no reason to ask his servants for forgiveness.

This analysis has a good deal to commend it. Almost all white South African children have bred in the bone the experience that there is always somebody cleaning, cooking, serving for them, and that this somebody is black. Before they consciously reflect on this situation, they have already absorbed the impression of standing above black people — a sense of superiority at the most profound emotional level, which is reinforced daily in school and church, in economic circles and social gatherings. For decades the apartheid system solidified these assumptions. Many churches justified them as ordained by God and prescribed by Scripture. So in the course of time the racial divisions came to appear natural and the system of townships did not strike people as profoundly grotesque.

Although segregation by law has now been abolished, inner segregation continues — and along with it all the anxieties about touching persons of the other race and the insecurities about how to relate to them, even among persons who mean well and who welcome the New South Africa.

It should be noted that the extent of racist formation is different for different generations. Members of the older generation, who were reared before the strict segregation was enforced, may have more relaxed racial relationships. Those most severely affected by the apartheid system seem to me to be those who were born in the 1950s and 1960s and never experienced an alternative. Again different is the emotional situation of the younger generation born after the Soweto uprisings in 1976, when the system began its long, slow process of disintegration.

How does one liberate the bosses from their racial captivity? This can happen only if and when some of them vicariously come forward to speak disarming and liberating words of repentance. Who is there in the white society who will find the redeeming words and pull down the barriers they have erected around themselves? Will the Dutch Reformed Church, which has been so close to the National Party, find the spiritual power to take this liberating step? A first step in this direction was undertaken by a group of Dutch Reformed clergy in Stellenbosch, who addressed the TRC with a confession of guilt. [5]

The dangers of amnesty

If there is no one to lead white South Africans out of the no-man's land of denial, the amnesty foreseen by the Act might well become a dangerous instrument.

Ill feelings were aroused on 11 October 1996 when the news went out that former defence minister Malan and nineteen others had been acquitted by the KwaZulu supreme court on an indictment of murdering thirteen persons, among them many women and children, in Kwamakutha, a township near Durban, in 1987. Many black South Africans bitterly interpreted the decision as a sign that even after the end of apartheid everything is meant to remain the same. In the courts the judges have not changed. In government offices the top civil servants are still white, as are the leaders in banks and businesses. Is this why the Reconstruction and Development Programme does not progress more quickly and the necessary economic changes are so abysmally slow?

No doubt, there is deep frustration among many black persons who have entered the new South Africa with high hopes. Archbishop Tutu is well aware of this growing uneasiness, of course. Again and again he has pointed out that the National Unity and Reconciliation Act is a compromise, and that all South Africans have to learn to live with compromises. "Remember what the alternative would have been!", he keeps saying. "If members of the police can convince the Amnesty Committee that they have made a full disclosure of their acts and that these were politically motivated, then they are entitled to amnesty. They don't even have to say that they feel sorry for what they have done. This is hard to swallow."

But persons like Archbishop Tutu would also acknowledge how difficult it is to make a full and public disclosure. To admit guilt even in the privacy of one's own home is not easy. How much more difficult to reveal one's involvement in the most heinous crimes before the eyes of the entire nation! And how difficult to name superiors and colleagues and thereby to "betray" and "desert" one's comrades! It takes considerable determination and courage to break rank and to leave the circle of subtle threats and compensations. A considerable portion of the implicated police and security forces still seem to be trying to protect themselves and the system in the hope of somehow managing to avoid the TRC and the courts.

It is reasonable to admonish citizens to live with compromises. At the same time, it must be understood that the anger of disadvantaged and victimized human beings will only increase if their oppressors seem to be getting away with their evil acts while they themselves continue to wait for decent houses, jobs and professional training. The acceptance of amnesties will largely depend on the measure in which the needs of the victims are being met. There must be a clear willingness on the part of the white South African society to make amends in unequivocal terms. If these are not forthcoming, the work of the TRC might well appear as a strategy to placate people's feelings rather than to heal their bitter wounds.

Healing the past

Why is it that most black South Africans cannot share the attitude so widely taken by whites: "Let bygones be bygone"? When white business people say that they accept the new constitution of South Africa as the basis for opening a new chapter in their nation's history, they are not necessarily engaging in an act of amnesia. They are simply acting out of a disposition that is typical of Western European culture, which regards the past as over and finished. Europeans may honour their dead, but they do not live with the awareness that the spirits of the dead are still with them and that it is vitally important to reconcile the unredeemed spirits of the past.

But this is a conviction deeply rooted in black African spirituality — that there can be no peaceful present as long as the spirits of the dead are not laid to rest. Many relatives of murdered or disappeared persons have asked the TRC to help them to get back from the police the remains of their loved ones, so that they can bury them in a decent and dignified manner. The burial is the ritual by which a lost member of the family can finally be brought home. This is the way the harmony between the generations is restored and maintained.

This spirituality should not be dismissed as "naïve" or "pagan" but recognized as a worldview that knows something of the fundamental connectedness of all life. Each individual human being is seen as a member of a community which includes the past and the coming generations. Coming to terms with the past is more than a matter of settling legal claims; it is an act of re-membering, of bringing together what belongs together. It has a great deal to do with healing, redemption and liberation.

In the heritage of African peoples there are concepts and rituals that endow the notion of reconciliation with profound meaning. Often reference is made to *ubuntu*, a term which connotes the basic connectedness of all human beings beyond all lines of race and class. Concepts like these help African peoples to transcend the violent mechanisms of denial and retaliation that typify Western cultures.

Are white people in South Africa prepared to see the TRC as an opportunity to get a deeper grasp of the spiritual power of their black fellow-citizens? Will they learn from them to work for processes of re-membering, of bringing peace to the past for the sake of the present and the future? Will they grasp the victims' readiness to forgive them as a chance to leave the prisons of shame and the dungeons of denial?

The haunting remark of a black clergyman in Alan Paton's famous novel *Cry the Beloved Country* should not be forgotten: "I have one great fear in my heart — that one day when they turn to loving they will find that we are turned to hating."

Elements of a politics of reconciliation

As the name of the Act suggests, the work of the TRC is to serve national unity by transcending the divisions of the past so that similar violations of human rights may be avoided in the future. Thus its function is not only cathartic but also preparatory and educative. In that sense, it is a central element in the building of a "rainbow nation".

It is clear that the TRC has only a limited mandate. During the short time-span provided by the Act, the commission will only be able to provide a set of recommendations; and a great deal of its success will depend on how these are incorporated into the overall policies of the new South Africa. In order to outline this wider context the following considerations appear necessary:

The primacy of the judiciary

Despite the widespread disappointment over the outcome of the Malan trial, the relevance of law for constructing a dependable social order must be affirmed. By establishing the TRC the South African government made a conscious decision not to pursue apartheid crimes according to the manner of the Nuremberg and Tokyo war tribunals. This must not be understood as a lessening of the authority of the law; indeed, the stability of the country will depend to a large degree on the absolute sovereignty of and public confidence in the legal order. This is the most important way to avoid private and ethnic feuds, mob-rule and the further spread of violence.

The culture of violence created by the long decades of apartheid did not miraculously disappear with the demise of its legal framework and ideological justifications. There have always been links between politically motivated violence and criminal violence. Furthermore, systemic impoverishment provokes "horizontal violence" in all its forms, in the home, on the streets and in the drugs and arms trade. To blame the present government for the increase of violent crime and to overlook the decades of institutionalized violence, which have served as a veritable training camp of violence in which there were many able students, is cynical and unjustified.

Working for the primacy of the law is thus an eminent task not only for the state but also for the general public and all sectors of civil society. A great deal of monitoring will be needed regarding the appointment of judges, public prosecutors and police officers. Respect for the law and a sense of personal decency must also be developed to curb corruption.

A special problem for South Africa is how to deal with persons who seek political office although they have been deeply involved in apartheid. The earlier practice of "banning" persons whose public activity is not desired is not advisable. But the media and other agents of civil society should resolutely monitor all who seek positions of leadership in politics, economics, the judiciary and public administration. The vitality of any democracy depends on vigorous control of those who seek an official mandate.

The restoring face of justice

The first few months of the TRC's work made abundantly clear that its greatest service consists in restoring the dignity of the victims. We have mentioned earlier how important it is to make visible the stories of those who were destined to be invisible and to integrate their witness into the memory of the nation. This is a process of immense symbolic significance, though this symbolism can evaporate quickly if it is not nurtured by tangible and practical acts of compensation.

This orientation to the victim must be regarded as a positive contribution to our concept of justice. The classical judicial system is marked by its orientation towards the culprit, because the guilt of the perpetrator must be proved beyond any reasonable doubt. In the TRC hearings, the suffering and hurt persons are given full attention. The restoration of their dignity is considered as important for the good of society as the punishment of the guilty.

Placing the restorative and constructive element of justice alongside the punitive element should be repeated in other countries. It is a sad fact that there was never anything equivalent to a TRC in Germany to account for the Nazi crimes. All attention focused on the punitive aspect — through the Nuremberg trials and subsequent court cases. It is also evident that the Hague tribunal set up in the aftermath of war crimes in the former Yugoslavia will lead at best to a very marginal realization of punitive justice. It can do very little to restore the dignity of those people who have suffered pain and humiliation.

This attention to the restorative side of justice must be accompanied by the aspect of compensation. This again brings us face to face with the question of whether it is at all possible to compensate for injustices suffered. What kind of restitution is imaginable in dealing with murder, disappearances or torture without constituting an added humiliation?

Since the wheel of history cannot be turned back, there can be no restitution in the strict sense of the term. Therefore, we might identify a double focus to restoring the dignity of the victims. The healing of the personal dignity — the restoration of the personhood of the victim — is directed towards the past and requires symbolic acts. Material and social assistance must be directed towards the future. It must aim at securing equal opportunity for persons who have been marginalized; in other words, it must seek to build up their capacity to have a future worthy of the name. Hence the process of reconciliation is not interested only in past grievances. By way of looking at the past, it tries to effect the inauguration of more just conditions for the future.

Distributive justice

This leads directly to a third aspect of justice, commonly called distributive justice. As we talk about securing equal opportunities for the disadvantaged, we must also reflect on how those who benefited from injustice can restore their stolen gains. Equality is not possible without equalization.

Earlier I mentioned that the National Unity and Reconciliation Act stipulates the establishment of a President's Fund out of which compensations will have to be paid. It appears questionable that this will be practicable in view of the sheer number of claims. But there is a more fundamental question. Should the restoration of the victims of apartheid be met by payments from the privy purse of the president? Is this not a task that requires a nationwide process which clearly and significantly links together the beneficiaries and the victims of apartheid?

It may be appropriate in this context to refer to the Equalization of Burdens Acts (*Lastenausgleichsgesetze*) passed by the governments in the Federal Republic of Germany since 1952. Their object was to oblige citizens whose houses, estates, factories and the like had survived the war relatively unscathed to cede a large portion of their value to the state for a period of 30 years. This enabled the government to organize large-scale resettlement, compensation and housing programmes for the millions of refugees and others who had suffered severely during the war. The criterion of renunciation was used as a necessary component for the construction of social justice.

A similar approach would seem appropriate in South Africa. The apartheid system granted the white part of the South African population material, social and professional advantages which have largely been paid for by the oppression and exploitation of the black majority. There is a direct correlation between the wealth of the whites and the poverty of the blacks. So as the new South Africa contemplates processes to create equal opportunities for all its citizens, it cannot do so without programmes of renunciation for those who have gained most. Verbal confessions of guilt are not worth much unless they are matched by concrete forms of renunciation. This seems to be one of the deepest challenges for a peaceful transition in South Africa.

So far the costs of the process of transition have been borne by the majority of the people and by their stupendous capacity of forgiveness and forbearance. But if the beneficiaries of apartheid seek to carry over their advantages into the new South Africa without being ready to let go of some of their wealth — for instance, in the form of land — then it is safe to say that the patience will eventually be exhausted and violence increase even further.

The capacity to create a better future for the "rainbow nation" will depend on the willingness of the powerful to share. Thus the government's ambitious Reconstruction and Development Programme is the practical expression of truth and reconciliation. It would be a fateful illusion to separate the urgent tasks in the fields of economics, professional training, social and health care, employment policies and ecology from the follow-up processes of the apartheid period.

It is appropriate to refer in this connection to South Africa's external debt. The new South African government had to honour the debts incurred by the apartheid régime to the International Monetary Fund, World Bank, national governments and commercial banks. But it must be asked whether it is just to burden coming generations with the debts of a criminal and corrupt government. Such a financial policy confirms a state of irreconciliation which might well render the efforts of the TRC null and void. What price is the international community prepared to pay for the abolition of a system it consistently condemned in thousands of statements and resolutions?

Structures of symbolic communication

So far I have sketched some of the legal, social, economic and political consequences of the TRC's work. Finally, I want to mention an aspect which at first glance may seem to be of little practical use. Yet it might well be of significant importance for the national unity of

South Africa. There needs to be a *symbolic communication* about truth and reconciliation.

How the final report of the TRC is received will be of utmost importance. One might imagine a public ritual similar to the one employed by Chilean President Aylwin, who presented the report of the commission dealing with the crimes of the Pinochet era on television to the Chilean people and the victim community in particular, asking them for forgiveness in the name of the country. What would it mean if President Mandela, in the name of the republic, and accompanied by a group of significant national leaders, presented the TRC's report to the citizens and asked all the victims for forgiveness?

At the same time a national Remembrance Day might be instituted. It could be celebrated in different ways in various parts of the country according to local needs and preferences. Some cities may wish to build apartheid-museums and memorials for the victims. Obviously new textbooks must be written for the schools — a process that has already begun — to pave the way for walking together through the histories of the South African peoples. This will contribute to a process of deep remembering which transcends racial stereotypes and enemy images.

Much of this work can be done by sectors of civil society, including the churches. So far many churches have devoted a great deal of energy to religiously stabilizing the identities of their separate communities. This has created misunderstanding and mistrust even among those whose doctrinal basis was identical, severely hindering the advance of their joint ecumenical vocation.

Now is a *kairos*, a blessed and critical moment, for the creation of local covenants and schemes of cooperation to heal the deep divisions that mark South African society. There is need to work for ministries of trust after so many years of distrust and hatred — a task that requires a great deal of patience and openness to the Spirit of life.

Challenges to the international community

The unprecedented TRC process merits close international attention by persons involved in peace research, legal questions, religious studies, theology, social psychology and other disciplines. It will be especially important to seek possibilities of transferring this process to other conflict areas. Significantly, some members of the TRC have been invited to visit Rwanda in order to advise the government how to deal with the aftermath of the genocide between Hutus and Tutsis. Many other conflict areas could be helped by an approach similar to the TRC.

The success of the TRC will depend largely on how quickly some of South Africa's most pressing problems can be met. The townships are time-bombs that need immediate attention. Unemployment is rampant, and the disparities between the small elites and poor masses are flagrant. It is urgent to establish policies of social reform.

It is disquieting that the neo-liberal and monetarist adjustment schemes which dominate international politics today are not interested in national development strategies that are essentially guided by social welfare-state approaches. The global approach of the financial markets does not leave space for national programmes of restoring and healing. So the international ideological context is not conducive to meeting the pressing internal needs of South Africa.

While many around the world have praised the miraculous change that has taken place under Nelson Mandela, these are empty words unless they are matched by practical solidarity. This applies not only to national governments and international political and financial corporations; it also applies to international non-governmental organizations, the trade unions, churches and similarly engaged popular agencies. They too are called to ensure that the historic experiment of the South African people turns out to be a success.

It is not only the peace of the new South Africa that is at stake here. The approach of the TRC is relevant all over the world. It is a challenge to the so-called realists who say that the only criterion for politics should be the interests of the nations. But what is in the best interests of the people? Can values such as truth, reconciliation and unity be branded as idealistic or even romantic? The South African approach is an important experiment in relating ethics to politics. It does so essentially by integrating the story of the victims into the formulation of political goals and interests. It does not accept the modern creed that the winner takes it all. The "winner syndrome" of today creates victims on all sides.

The world is getting too small for that kind of politics. The lesson South Africa is trying to teach us is that by turning to the victims and restoring their dignity, a space is created in which lasting peace can build its home.

NOTES

[1] What is here can be only an interim analysis, completed in January 1997 and reflecting only on the TRC's first six months of work. My comments are based on two 1996 visits to South Africa: in April to East London, Durban, Cape Town and Johannesburg, in October to Pietermaritzburg, Grahamstown, Aliwal North, Pretoria and Johannesburg. I am deeply grateful to the South African Council of Churches for inviting me to attend various sessions of the TRC and to participate in nationwide conferences on its relevance for the churches and other sections of civil society.

[2] Republic of South Africa, *Government Gazette*, Vol. 361, no. 16579, Cape Town, 26 July 1995, ch. 2. The cutoff date was originally set for December 1993; subsequently the TRC itself suggested a prolongation to 10 May 1994 (the day President Mandela took office), which would thus include acts of violence committed prior to the first general elections, held on 27 April 1994. The government has agreed to make this amendment.

[3] Regarding the practical details of the work of the TRC, the following may be helpful:

1. The TRC has 17 members, elected by a special committee not on the basis of party affiliation but on their personal merits and moral integrity. Former Anglican archbishop and Nobel peace laureate Desmond Tutu was elected chair of the TRC; his deputy is Alex Boraine, a well-known white theologian and politician.

2. The Act establishes three committees — on human rights violations, on amnesty and on reparation and rehabilitation. Each has five members: two are from the TRC, the others are suitable experts in these fields. Because of the far-reaching powers of the Amnesty Committee, it is set up like a judicial court.

3. The TRC's "investigating unit" processes all applications, conducts background research, inspects archives and prepares the materials for the hearings. Only about 10 percent of the persons presenting their cases are dealt with in public hearings, with their consent.

4. It is not yet clear how many cases will be presented; suggested figures have ranged as high as fifty to one hundred thousand.

5. The Act gives the TRC 18 months to finish its work and another three months to prepare a final report. The president must then present the report to the public and pass it over to parliament within two months. In this context, measures must be taken to settle the claims for reparation and rehabilitation; and the Act foresees establishment of a "President's Fund" to make the necessary compensations.

6. The TRC has set up regional offices in Cape Town, Johannesburg, East London and Durban to facilitate processing of applications and direct contact with persons and institutions involved.

[4] Cf. esp. Robert J. Lifton, *The Life of the Self: Toward a New Psychology*, New York, Simon & Schuster, 1976; *The Broken Connection: On Death and the Continuity of Life*, New York, Basic Books, 1983; *The Future of Immortality and Other Essays for a Nuclear Age*, New York, Basic Books, 1987.

[5] In this context it is important to remember the Rustenburg Declaration of November 1990, which had at its centre a confession of sin made by a national conference of church leaders in South Africa. The Rustenburg Declaration was a milestone in the churches' struggle against apartheid, though its practical implications have not yet been fully met. Cf. L. Alberts and F. Chikane, *The Road to Rustenburg: The Church Looking Forward to a New South Africa*, Cape Town, Struik Christian Books, 1991, pp.275ff.

Appendix

An Art That Can Be Learned

Summary of a Seminar with Body Exercises

In May 1993 I was approached by Elsa Tamez of the Seminario Bíblico Latinoamericano in San José, Costa Rica, to conduct a four-hour seminar on "forgiveness". She had heard of my interest in this subject and wanted to integrate it in her own seminar on "Reconciliation and Justice". I accepted the invitation with some trepidation; for I knew that it would be difficult to explain what *perdón* meant to me. Elsa's students — some twenty women and men — came from all parts of Latin America. Many had already been working in their churches, most of which are very small and poor. They bore in their lives the heavy burdens of a history of oppression and exploitation, notably by European nations. How could I as a European speak to them about forgiveness?

To remain as close as possible to their experience, I decided to conduct three body exercises and to engage the students in an exchange. From my earlier exposure to this type of work, I knew that what one experiences in the flesh usually has a deep impact on one's thinking. Body work prevents persons from merely theorizing about theological problems and enables them to situate their insights in their immediate biographical context. Since forgiveness has to do with intensely intimate experiences and feelings, it seemed appropriate to use such an approach, even though it was unfamiliar to most of them. But they participated with the greatest enthusiasm.

In the following summary, based on my recollections, I have changed the names of the students.

Exercise 1

To create an open space in the seminar room we moved the tables and chairs along the walls. I invited the students to move freely about the room and make contacts with the others, not by speaking but through looks and gestures.

After some brief initial hesitation, there was a lot of movement in the room. Eye-contact was the most important medium for establishing relationships. Some embraced each other, walked about for a while hand in hand, then separated. Others were more reserved, expressing the distance between each other by merely nodding. But on the whole there was an active exchange among all members of the group.

After about five minutes I closed the exercise and invited the students to sit around in a circle. I asked them: "What have we done just now?"

"It was nice," they said, "but so what?" While it was good to be in contact with so many persons, there was nothing special about it. It had been a very normal situation, with experiences of closeness and distance, warmth and also some reserve.

This experience of normality seems to me to be necessary to understand the two following exercises better.

Exercise 2

I divided the students into two groups and told both to move about in the room as before. Group A, however, had the assignment of "subduing" Group B through a symbolic gesture of submission. From that moment on, both parties were to move around the room as before, but all members of Group B had to move on their knees while Group A had to walk tiptoe. As in the first exercise, there would be no talking. When a signal was given, the members of Group A turned against the members of Group B and "oppressed" them. There was some resistance, but after a brief struggle the members of group B were crawling on their knees and the "victors" in Group A were walking tiptoe. Very quickly the atmosphere in the room changed dramatically. The movements were slow, the eye contacts between members of the two opposing groups awkward and even hostile, the contacts between members of the same groups embarrassed and uncertain. The good-humoured ease of the previous exercise had disappeared entirely.

When I asked the members of Group B to share their experiences, they talked about the physical discomfort of crawling on their knees. They needed to concentrate on their situation in order to come to terms with it. There was anger and shame against the "oppressors".

When Group A was asked to share, they mentioned first how awkward and stiff it felt to have to walk tiptoe. Forced to be preoccupied with their own movements, they were less willing to have contacts with their "peers".

I then related this experience to the theme of forgiveness, which emerges as a problem only in situations like this, when violent and unjust actions have disrupted relationships and destroyed the original equality. Oppression corresponds with self-aggrandizement. Walking tiptoe indicated that the members of Group A had made themselves bigger than they really were, while members of Group B were humiliated to a status that did not do justice to their original height. The great variety of contacts which typified Exercise 1 had been drastically reduced. Those who walk tiptoe can only look down on those who crawl on their knees. Those who are made low can only look up to the others. There is no chance for embraces.

Note that this new situation is felt to be painful by members of both groups. The former spontaneity has been replaced by constrained artificiality.

In interpreting this experience theologically, we see that the kind of domination exercised by Group A becomes guilt because it is based on stolen power. This kind of domination depends on the power that is taken from the others. It enables the powerful to make themselves bigger than they really are. Impotence is understood as a loss of original strength, leading to feelings of shame because one's real height has been violently reduced. The oppressed not only feel pain but also experience a profound sense of embarrassment and humiliation. Poverty is more than material want; it goes along with shame and produces feelings of helpless fury.

The students related this group experience to the social and political realities in which they live. They knew that the wealth of the powerful is built on the poverty and humiliation of the poor. Some of the members of Group A also remarked how tempting it is to use the power to oppress others and how quickly one becomes part of situations of domination.

Exercise 3

What would forgiveness between members of the two groups look like? I asked three members of each group to form a pair with a member of the other group and to act out possible solutions — again without talking.

In the play of the first pair, Maria (Group B) moved on her knees close to Pablo (Group A). With desperate movements she implored him to liberate her from her painful situation. He tried to get away from her, but she followed him with outstretched arms. At last he turned to her, bent over and lifted her to her feet. They smiled at each other briefly and returned to their seats.

In the second play, Martín (B) and Jorge (A) had only very scant eye contact. Martín, totally caught up in his position, stared at the ground and barely moved. Jorge stood very stiffly, seeming not to notice the man on his knees. Minutes passed with both actors barely moving. The group followed this "interaction" in anxious silence. At last I terminated this play. Jorge and Martín sat down again.

In the third play Lidia (B) moved slowly towards Juan (A). He did not try to avoid her. She looked at him and he faced her look. Then Lidia touched Juan's foot very lightly. Juan dropped to his knees in front of her. They looked at each other for a long time. Then they began to smile, embraced each other and drew themselves to their feet again. Arm in arm they walked about for a short while before returning to their seats.

When I asked Maria and Pablo to interpret their play, Maria said, "I was suffering so much that I had to implore Pablo with all my remaining energies to help me get back on my feet. That is why I insisted so desperately on contacting him." Pablo added, "It was embarrassing for me to experience Maria moving so close to me all the time. So I bowed down to her and put her up again. But I did not really want to do it."

Then I asked the entire group to share its impressions. Someone said, "It cannot be called forgiveness when humiliated persons have to beg their oppressors to lift them to their feet again. Does the victim have to beg to be forgiven? Surely it cannot be called forgiveness if the perpetrator bows down condescendingly to his victims and lifts them up. Forgiveness must be something different from an affable favour!"

I asked Jorge and Martín to express their feelings. Martín replied: "I was so absorbed in my pain and anger that I felt neither the strength nor the will to look at Jorge or to give him a sign that I needed his help. The longer the scene lasted and the more I noticed that Jorge was not making a move, the more the resentment and stiffness grew within me." Jorge said, "I enjoyed my superior position. I sensed Martín's resentment and enmity, so I did not make any move in his direction. I ought to have done something, but my pride would not let me."

The other students added their reactions. "It was horrible to witness the block between the two." One person spoke of wanting to enter the scene and shake them into action. There was no forgiveness in this interaction. It was recognized that the brief eye contact between the two at the beginning was not enough to cause a change in their relationship. Jorge ought to have made a move, but he could not bring himself to doing anything. The more time passed, the greater became the enmity between them. Obviously one can grow immobile in one's unwillingness to repent.

When I invited Lidia and Juan to talk about their experience, Juan said, "I sensed that I had to do something. When Lidia moved towards me, I went to her. Then I noticed that she gave me a sign. She touched my foot, and I knew that I had to kneel down in front of her to get into contact with her again. It was immensely liberating to be able to look each other in the eye again. After that, it was clear that we would help each other to get on our feet again and to walk about awhile."

Lidia added: "I did not intend to beg, but I wanted him to understand that I was waiting for his action and that I would be prepared to react affirmatively. That is why I tapped on his shoes."

When the seminar group commented on this scene they noted that forgiveness between Lidia and Juan began in the moment that he dropped to his knees and they could look at each other face to face. Juan gave up his supremacy, and they helped each other to get to their feet again and then walked together. Lidia's small sign gave Juan the confidence that his act of disclosure would be accepted. That is why he dared to kneel down before her. Without this sign he might have behaved like Jorge in the earlier play.

Theological interpretation

After a break, we sat down in the circle again to discuss these three acts theologically. "The first two scenes gave us the impression that there was no forgiveness," I said. "What was it in the play of Lidia and Juan that made us think that this was in fact forgiveness?"

We noted that forgiveness begins with the party who has stolen power giving up this dominant position. It renounces false power and humiliates itself voluntarily. The perpetrator wants to get where the victim is. What we traditionally call repentance is the recognition that there must be a renunciation of presumed supremacy, a kind of disarmament, for it will be intolerable in the long run to live with this stolen supremacy, not only for the victim, but also for the perpetrator. Repentance implies getting on the same level with the victim, at least for a moment. Juan and Lidia do not remain on their knees forever. They lift each other to their feet — which means that they help each other to resume their original stature. Only together can they regain the human height that had been theirs before. Only then can they walk together and do things together. Forgiveness does not mean that Juan has to crawl on his knees while Lidia lords over him. It has nothing do to with simply exchanging roles but has to do with regaining a genuine human dignity.

Lidia has played an important part. Through her looks, and especially through her sign, she has given Juan the assurance that she was willing to forgive, that she would not turn away when he knelt in front of her, that she would accept his gesture of self-humiliation as the beginning of a new story together.

It is impossible to interpret the first play as forgiveness, because Pablo had not given up his supremacy. His help was only an act of condescension in order to get rid of the nuisance Maria was causing him. Condescension must not be mistaken for forgiveness. Even if Pablo's act means that Maria is no longer on her knees, it has not led to a new community between the two. Maria owes her new freedom to his clemency, and that means she has not really gained her dignity as an equal human person. Pablo is still on tiptoe, as it were. Help without repentance may have some equalizing effect, but it is not forgiveness.

Finally we raised the question of why it had gone so well in the third scene between Lidia and Juan. Why did Jorge and Martín get stuck in their hostility? To what extent does forgiveness depend on the disposition and character of persons?